Ontic

Ontic
A Knowledge Representation System for Mathematics

David A. McAllester

The MIT Press
Cambridge, Massachusetts
London, England

This book was printed and bound in the United States of America

Library of Congress Cataloging-in-Publication Data

McAllester, David A.
    Ontic: a knowledge representation system for
mathematics

    (The MIT Press series in artificial intelligence)
    Includes index.
    1. Automatic theorem proving. 2. Ontic (Computer
system) I. Title. II. Series.
QA76.9.A96M37 1988   510'.28'563   88-8090
ISBN 0-262-13235-4

Contents

Series Foreword

Artificial intelligence is the study of intelligence using the ideas and methods of computation. Unfortunately, a definition of intelligence seems impossible at the moment because intelligence appears to be an amalgam of so many information-processing and information-representation abilities.

Of course psychology, philosophy, linguistics, and related disciplines offer various perspectives and methodologies for studying intelligence. For the most part, however, the theories proposed in these fields are too incomplete and too vaguely stated to be realized in computational terms. Something more is needed, even though valuable ideas, relationships, and constraints can be gleaned from traditional studies of what are, after all, impressive existence proofs that intelligence is in fact possible.

Artificial intelligence offers a new perspective and a new methodology. Its central goal is to make computers intelligent, both to make them more useful and to understand the principles that make intelligence possible. That intelligent computers will be extremely useful is obvious. The more profound point is that artificial intelligence aims to understand intelligence using the ideas and methods of computation, thus offering a radically new and different basis for theory formation. Most of the people doing work in artificial intelligence believe that these theories will apply to any intelligent information processor, whether biological or solid state.

There are side effects that deserve attention, too. Any program that will successfully model even a small part of intelligence will be inherently massive and complex. Consequently, artificial intelligence continually confronts the limits of computer-science technology. The problems encountered have been hard enough and interesting enough to seduce artificial intelligence people into working on them with enthusiasm. It is natural, then, that there has been a steady flow of ideas from artificial intelligence to computer science, and the flow shows no sign of abating.

The purpose of The MIT Press Series in Artificial Intelligence is to provide people in many areas, both professionals and students, with timely, detailed information about what is happening on the frontiers in research centers all over the world.

J. Michael Brady
Daniel G. Bobrow
Randall Davis

Acknowledgments

This manuscript is a heavily revised version of my Ph.D. dissertation written at the MIT Artificial Intelligence Laboratory. My thesis would never have been completed without the unending encouragement of my thesis supervisor Gerald Sussman. Albert Meyer forced me to clarify my thinking and to demonstrate the utility of my ideas by constructing a working system. Jonathan Rees provided stimulating discussions and useful feedback as the first user of the Ontic formal language. Robert Constable, Yishai Feldman, Bob Givan, Chet Murthy, Peter Szolovits, and Ramin Zabih, read and commented on early drafts. Michael O'Donnell provided detailed technical comments that greatly improved the final version. I also owe thanks to members of the MIT Artificial Intelligence Laboratory and the Cornell Computer Science Department for providing a stimulating research environment in which the ideas in this book developed.

Preface

Before the dawn of the field of artificial intelligence Alan Turing proposed a test that could be used to determine whether or not a given machine could think like a person. His test involves a room containing two computer terminals. One terminal is connected to the machine. When a question, posed in English, is typed on that terminal the machine must respond by typing an answer in English. The other terminal will also answer questions posed in English, but these questions are actually answered by a person sitting in another room. We are given the task of determining which terminal is connected to the machine and which to the person. To determine which is the machine we may ask *any question whatsoever* at either terminal. After asking as many questions as we like, we must guess which is the machine and which the person. If it is not possible to do better than chance in guessing which is the machine, the machine is thinking. This has become known as the Turing test of machine thought.

Can computers be made to think? No definitive answer to this question has emerged during the first thirty years of research in artificial intelligence. No machine today can even approach passing the Turing test. It is even hard to determine which of the many research areas in AI are most relevant to building such a machine. I have come to the conclusion that at this time the greatest progress toward passing the Turing test can be made by attempting to automate conceptual mathematical reasoning. This is, of course, a very controversial position within artificial intelligence. Many researchers believe that mathematical thought is a rare phenomenon among humans and not relevant to everyday intelligent activity. While this may be true, to build a machine that does conceptual mathematics one must develop mechanisms that are useful for general intelligent activity. In particular, automating conceptual mathematical reasoning requires storing and *effectively using* large quantities of knowledge in the form of mathematical definitions, lemmas and theorems. I believe that knowledge representation and techniques for effectively using large conceptual knowledge bases are of central importance in the quest to pass the Turing test.

The goal of passing the Turing test is not the only reason to study automated conceptual mathematics. A machine that could efficiently verify natural mathematical arguments could be used to greatly increase our confidence in new mathematical results. Such a machine might also prove invaluable in verifying computer hardware and software. An automated reasoning system may someday greatly improve the effectiveness of compilers for computer programming languages, especially for highly parallel machines. Automated mathematical reasoning systems may some day play a central role in mathematical education. Such a system could be used to answer student questions and to verify student arguments. An effective automated mathematical reasoning system would have varied applications, many of which may not be foreseeable at this time.

Ambitious goals, such as passing the Turing test or constructing computers that create significant new mathematics, are well beyond the current capabilities of artificial intelligence. No one can predict when, if ever, such goals will be achieved. I feel, however, that in spite of the poverty of our current knowledge, it is now possible to uncover general principles of knowledge representation and machine inference that will ultimately prove significant in achieving the grand goals of AI. This book is the outcome of an attempt to find some such general principles of intelligence.

I AN OVERVIEW OF ONTIC

1 Ontic in Brief

Ontic is a computer system for verifying mathematical arguments. Starting with only the axioms of Zermelo-Fraenkel set theory, including Zorn's lemma as a version of the axiom of choice, the Ontic system has been used to define concepts involving partial orders and lattices and to verify a proof of the Stone representation theorem for Boolean lattices. This theorem involves an ultrafilter construction and is similar in complexity to the Tychonoff theorem in topology which states that an arbitrary product of compact spaces is compact. The individual steps in the proof were verified with an automated theorem prover. The Ontic theorem prover automatically accesses a lemma library containing hundreds of mathematical facts; as more facts are added to the system's lemma library the system becomes capable of verifying larger inference steps.

The Ontic theorem prover is based on what I call object-oriented inference. Object-oriented inference is a forward chaining inference process applied to a large lemma library and guided by a set of *focus objects*. The focus objects are terms in the sense of first order predicate calculus; they are expressions which denote objects. It is well known that unrestricted forward chaining starting with a large lemma library leads to an immediate combinatorial explosion. However, the Ontic theorem prover is guided by the focus objects; the inference process is restricted to statements that are, in a technical sense, about the focus objects. Thus the inference process is "object-oriented". In verifying an argument the user specifies the set of focus objects. For example the user may tell the system to consider an arbitrary lattice L, an arbitrary subset S of L, and an arbitrary member x of S. Ontic's inference mechanisms are restricted to a finite set of formulas that are about the given focus objects. Certain forward chaining constraint propagation techniques can be effectively applied to this finite set of formulas. Natural language mathematical arguments, like those found in textbooks and journals, appear to be object-oriented in the sense that they instruct the reader to focus on certain objects. Thus Ontic's object-oriented inference mechanisms seem well suited for verifying natural arguments.

There are two motivations for building a system for verifying natural arguments. First there is an engineering motive: a sufficiently powerful mechanical verifier could have a variety of important practical applications, such as ensuring the correctness of mathematical arguments, the correctness of software systems, and the correctness of engineered devices in general. Second, the construction of a verification system for natural arguments can be motivated in terms of cognitive psychology. A verification system for natural arguments provides a computational model of the human cognitive processes involved in verifying arguments. The plausibility of such a cognitive model can be judged by comparing the length and structure of the arguments acceptable to people with the length and structure of arguments acceptable to the cognitive model.

The engineering motive and the cognitive model motive for building verification systems are not independent; a verification system that is a good cognitive model is likely to be pragmatically useful. More specifically, a verification system is a good cognitive model to the extent that arguments acceptable to the model are similar to the arguments acceptable to people. Thus if a verification system is a good cognitive model then it should be easy to convert arguments that are acceptable to people to arguments that can be verified by the system; a system that is a good cognitive model provides a good "impedance match" between the human user and the verification system.

On the other hand, the two motivations for verification systems, the engineering motive and the cognitive model motive, are different motivations with different criteria for success. A verification system that exhibits clearly superhuman performance in its ability to verify statements is a bad cognitive model but a good verifier from an engineering point of view. It turns out that Ontic's mechanism for reasoning about equality, congruence closure, leads to some clear examples of superhuman performance on the part of the Ontic system. Thus congruence closure is not a good cognitive model for the way people reason about equality—there are equality reasoning mechanisms which are weaker than congruence closure which provide better cognitive models. However, from an engineering point of view congruence closure is better than the weaker mechanism (at least on serial machines). The analysis of congruence closure as a cognitive model is presented in detail in chapter 3.

The Ontic system was designed with both motivations in mind—an attempt was made to make the system a pragmatically effective verification system and at the same time to make the system a rough model of human mathematical cognition. The Ontic system should be judged on two independent grounds relative to these two goals. First, one can evaluate the system as an engineered device for verifying proofs by attempting to use the system for that purpose. Second, one can attempt to evaluate the system as a cognitive model by judging the similarity between natural language arguments acceptable to people and formal arguments acceptable to the system.

The remainder of this chapter is divided into four sections. The first section briefly discusses natural language mathematical arguments. The second section of the chapter discusses the formal language used in the Ontic system. The third section describes the user-level interface to the system and gives several examples of arguments verified by the system. The fourth section describes the object-oriented inference mechanisms in more detail.

Ontic's relationship to previous work in reasoning, knowledge representation, and theorem proving is discussed in detail in chapter 2. Chapter 3 presents an analysis of the Ontic system as a cognitive model giving examples of both superhuman and subhuman performance on the part of the Ontic system. Chapter 4 gives a mathematically precise definition of the Ontic formal language. Chapter 5 gives inference rules that define the proof theory of the Ontic language. Chapter 6 gives technical details of the Ontic implementation. Chapter 7 lists some potential applications of automated inference systems such as Ontic and chapter 7 summarizes the main features of the Ontic system.

1.1 The Nature of Natural Arguments

By a "natural mathematical argument" I mean a proof written in a natural language, such as English, that would be acceptable as a fully worked out proof in a textbook or journal article. A natural mathematical argument consists of a sequence of natural language statements and the human reader is expected to use his or her knowledge and intelligence to see that each step clearly and necessarily follows from the previous steps. As an example of a natural argument consider the following proof that the square root of 2 is irrational.

Suppose that the square root of two were rational, i.e.

$$\frac{p^2}{q^2} = 2$$

The squares p^2 and q^2 must each have an even number of prime factors. Thus, if p^2/q^2 is an integer then this integer

must also have an even number of prime factors. But 2 has
only a single prime factor so p^2/q^2 cannot equal 2.

This argument is perfectly rigorous; every step clearly follows from
the previous steps and the conclusion is clearly established; $\sqrt{2}$ must
be irrational. However, understanding this argument requires knowing
certain facts about arithmetic and multisets. More specifically the above
argument implicitly rests on the following facts:

1. The fundamental theorem of arithmetic — every natural number has a
   unique multiset of prime factors.

2. The multiset of factors of p^2 is the multiset union of the prime factors
   of p with itself.

3. The multiset union of a multiset with itself has an even number of
   members (an even multiset cardinality).

4. If p/q is an integer then the multiset of prime factors of q must be a
   subset of the multiset of prime factors of p.

5. If p/q is an integer then the multiset of prime factors of p/q is the
   multiset difference of the prime factors of p and the prime factors of q.

6. If the multisets m_1 and m_2 both have an even number of members and
   m_2 is a subset of m_1 then the multiset difference of m_1 and m_2 has an
   even number of members.

The fundamental theorem of arithmetic is a deep theorem involving
several induction proofs. It seems quite likely that people have simply memorized this fact and use it freely. The other facts in the above
list have simpler proofs (given the fundamental theorem of arithmetic).
However, an explicit proof of any one of the above facts would be at
least as long as the above proof that the square root of 2 is irrational.
Furthermore, each of the above facts seems to be generally useful and
thus it seems likely, or at least plausible, that people have memorized
each of the above facts in addition to the fundamental theorem of arithmetic. People seem capable of using facts, such as the fundamental
theorem, unconsciously; when reading the above natural argument one
is not consciously aware of using the fundamental theorem of arithmetic.
The above example suggests that people verify mathematical arguments
by using knowledge they already have about the concepts involved and
by applying that knowledge unconsciously in verifying the steps of the
argument.

1.2 Ontic as a Formal Language

The Ontic system cannot read natural language—before an argument can be verified it must be translated into a machine readable form. The Ontic system manipulates formulas in the formal language called Ontic. The Ontic language is a syntactic sugar for first order set theory. The design of this syntactic sugar was driven by two motivations. First, the language is designed to be as similar as possible to natural language while still being simple and mathematically precise. Most atomic formulas in the Ontic language consists of a subject "noun phrase" and a predicate "verb phrase". In addition to being similar to natural language, the syntactic structure of the Ontic formal language facilitates the object-oriented inference mechanisms used in the system. Object-oriented inference is guided by a set of focus objects. The inference mechanisms "type" the focus objects—the system assigns a set of types to each focus object. In the Ontic system a type is any predicate of one argument; the types assigned to a focus object are predicates that are known to be true of that object. The syntax of the Ontic language is designed to facilitate this typing process; most atomic formulas state that a particular type applies to a particular object.

In the Ontic language there is no distinction between types, classes, sorts, and predicates of one argument. For an object x and type τ the phrases "τ contains x", "x is an instance of τ" and "τ is true of x" all mean the same thing. The word type is used, as opposed to the word class or predicate, because Ontic types are used in much the same way that types are used in computer programming languages; functions in the formal language can only be applied to arguments of the appropriate type and thus there is a distinction between "well-typed" and "ill-formed" expressions. For example, consider a function TOPOLOGICAL-CLOSURE such that if X is a topological space and A is a subset of X then the expression (TOPOLOGICAL-CLOSURE A X) denotes the topological closure of A as a subset of X. An application of the operator TOPOLOGICAL-CLOSURE is well typed just in case its second argument denotes a topological space and its first argument denotes a subset of that space. As an example of an expression that is not well typed, consider the expression (TOPOLOGICAL-CLOSURE X A) that results from providing the arguments in the wrong order: This is not well typed because A is not a topological space and X need not be a subset of A.

Rather than give a rigorous syntax and semantics for the Ontic language, this section discusses the language informally and largely by example. A more rigorous treatment is presented in chapter 4. Every expression of the Ontic language belongs to exactly one of five syntactic categories; an expression is either a term, a formula, a function expression, a type expression, or a type generator expression. Terms are expressions that denote objects.[1] A formula is an expression which denotes one of the Boolean truth values *true* or *false*.[2] A function expression denotes a mapping from objects to objects. Each function expression takes a fixed number of arguments and returns an object.[3] Type expressions are predicates of one argument.[4] A type generator expression denotes a mapping from objects to types. Each type generator expression takes a fixed number of arguments and returns a type.[5]

1.2.1   Types

Figure 1.1 lists some type expressions. The first five type expressions in figure 1.1 are type symbols. The types THING and SET are primitive type symbols in the Ontic system. The Ontic system allows for the possibility that there are instances of the universal type THING, such as symbols, which are not instances of the type SET. Each of the types GROUP, TOPOLOGICAL-SPACE, and RIEMANNIAN-MANIFOLD can be defined in terms of more primitive concepts. The next two type expressions are types that result from applying type generators to arguments. If a term s denotes a set then (MEMBER-OF s) is a type expression such that an object is an instance of the type (MEMBER-OF s) just in case it is a member of the set s.[6] Instances of the type expression (LOWER-BOUND-OF s p) are members of the partially ordered set p which are lower bounds of the subset s of p. One place lambda predicates are also type expressions. The instances of the type (LAMBDA ((x τ)) $\Phi(x)$) consist of exactly those instances x of the type τ which satisfy the formula $\Phi(x)$.

---

[1]A term is an expression of kind OBJECT. The rules of inference given in chapter 5 allow for the possibility that all objects are actually sets in a standard model of ZFC set theory. However, it is more natural, and equally consistent with the rules of inference, to assume that there exist objects that are not sets.

[2]A formula is an expression of kind BOOLEAN.

[3]Functions have kind OBJECT $\times$ OBJECT $\times$ $\cdots$ $\times$ OBJECT $\rightarrow$ OBJECT.

[4]Types have kind OBJECT $\rightarrow$ BOOLEAN.

[5]Type generators have kind OBJECT $\times$ OBJECT $\times$ $\cdots$ $\times$ OBJECT $\rightarrow$ TYPE.

[6]The term s denotes an object while the expression (MEMBER-OF s) denotes a type; no expression is allowed to be both a term and a type.

THING, SET, GROUP

TOPOLOGICAL-SPACE, RIEMANNIAN-MANIFOLD

(MEMBER-OF s), (LOWER-BOUND-OF s p)

(LAMBDA ((x τ)) $\Phi(x)$)

(EITHER x y)

(AND-TYPE τ_1 τ_2)

(OR-TYPE τ_1 τ_2)

Figure 1.1
Ontic Type Expressions

The type (EITHER X Y) contains only the instances X and Y. The type (AND-TYPE τ_1 τ_2) contains exactly those objects which are instances of both the types τ_1 and τ_2. The type (OR-TYPE τ_1 τ_2) contains exactly those objects which are instances of either of the types τ_1 or τ_2.

1.2.2 Terms

Figure 1.2 gives some Ontic terms. There are several ways of constructing terms in Ontic. The application of a function to arguments is a term. If τ is a "small" type expression then (THE-SET-OF-ALL τ) is a term which denotes the set of all instances of τ. The process of converting a type to a set is called *reification* and sets of the form (THE-SET-OF-ALL τ) are often called *reified types*. It is important to remember that there is a syntactic distinction between terms (which denote objects) and type expressions (which denote predicates). There are types, such as the type THING, which cannot be converted to sets— there is no set of all things. Most of the axioms of Zermelo-Fraenkel set theory state that certain sets exist. One can view these axioms as saying that certain types can be converted to sets. In the Ontic system these axioms of set theory are incorporated into the notion of a *syntactically small* type expression; the operator THE-SET-OF-ALL can only be applied to syntactically small type expressions. The notion of a syntactically small type expression, and the relation between this notion and the axioms of set theory, are discussed in more detail in chapter 4.

$(\mathit{fun}\ x_1\ x_2\ ...)$

(THE-SET-OF-ALL τ)

(THE-RULE fun)

(THE τ)

'symbol

Figure 1.2
Ontic Terms

If *fun* is a function of one argument then the term (THE-RULE *fun*)
denotes the "rule" that corresponds to the function. The relationship
between functions and rules is analogous to the relationship between
types and sets—the expression (THE-RULE *fun*) is a term and denotes
an object while *fun* is a function expression. Expressions of the form
(THE-RULE *fun*) are often referred to as *reified functions*. There exist
functions which cannot be reified as rules, e.g any function defined on
all sets, such as the function that maps an arbitrary set to its power set,
is too big to be reified as a rule.

If τ is a type with exactly one instance then the expression (THE τ)
is a term which denotes the single object contained in the type. For
example, let (PRIME-NUMBER-BETWEEN n m) be a type whose instances
are the prime numbers between n and m and consider the expression
(THE (PRIME-NUMBER-BETWEEN 20 25)). This expression denotes the
number 23.

Expressions of the form '*symbol* are also terms. For example the
expression 'FOO denotes the symbol FOO. Quoted symbols denote objects
which are instances of the type SYMBOL. The Ontic system allows for the
possibility that all objects are sets, i.e. that every object is an element of
a model of Zermelo-Fraenkel set theory. However, the Ontic system also
allows for a more natural interpretation under which rules and symbols
are not sets—the types SET, RULE, and SYMBOL can be assumed to be
disjoint.

1.2.3   Formulas

Figure 1.3 gives some Ontic formulas. The formula (IS x τ) is true just in case x denotes an instance of the type τ. Formulas of this form are intuitively pleasing because they seem to reflect natural language syntax—x is a subject "noun phrase" and the type τ is a predicate that applies to the subject. The formula (EXISTS-SOME τ) is true just in case there exists an instance of τ. More traditional quantification, such as (EXISTS ((x_1 τ_1) (x_2 τ_2) ...) $\Phi(x_1, x_2, ...)$) is also allowed. This formula is true just in case there exists instances $a_1, a_2 \ldots a_n$ of the types $\tau_1, \tau_2, \ldots \tau_n$ respectively such that such that Φ is true when the variables $x_1, x_2, \ldots x_n$ are interpreted as $a_1, a_2 \ldots a_n$ respectively. Of course, Ontic also provides for universally quantified formulas such as (FORALL ((x_1 τ_1) (x_2 τ_2) ...) $\Phi(x_1, x_2, ...)$). The formula (EXACTLY-ONE τ) is true just in case there is exactly one instance of the type τ. The formula (IS-EVERY τ_1 τ_2) is true just in case every instance of τ_1 is an instance of τ_2. Of course Boolean combinations of formulas are also formulas.

(IS x τ)

(EXISTS-SOME τ)

(EXISTS ((x_1 τ_1) (x_2 τ_2) ...) $\Phi(x_1, x_2, ...)$)

(FORALL ((x_1 τ_1) (x_2 τ_2) ...) $\Phi(x_1, x_2, ...)$)

(EXACTLY-ONE τ)

(IS-EVERY τ_1 τ_2)

(NOT Φ)

(AND Φ_1 Φ_2)

Figure 1.3
Ontic Formulas

1.2.4 Definitions

Figure 1.4 gives some examples of definitions of functions and type generators. Functions are defined with the DEFTERM construct as shown in the first example. In the first example POWER-SET is defined to be equivalent to the following lambda function.

```
(LAMBDA ((S SET)) (THE-SET-OF-ALL (SUBSET-OF S)))
```

Thus the function POWER-SET takes one argument which must be a set and returns the set of all subsets of that set. Types and type generators are defined with the DEFTYPE construct.

The second definition in figure 1.4 defines LOWER-BOUND-OF to be a type generator which takes two arguments: a set s and a poset p where the set s is required to be a subset of the set of elements of p. The type generator LOWER-BOUND-OF takes these arguments and returns a type: a predicate of one argument. An object x is an element of the type (LOWER-BOUND-OF s p) just in case x is an element of the underlying set of the poset p and every member of the set s is greater than or equal to x under the ordering imposed by the poset p. The type generator GREATEST-LOWER-BOUND-OF is similar to LOWER-BOUND: it takes a set s and a poset p where s is a subset of the underlying set of p and yields a type. An object x is an element of the type (GREATEST-LOWER-BOUND-OF s p) just in case x is a lower bound of s in the poset p and every lower bound of s in p is greater or equal to x. The type COMPLETE-LATTICE is defined so that an object p is of type COMPLETE-LATTICE just in case p is a poset such that for every subset s of the underlying set of p there exists a greatest lower bound of s under the ordering imposed by p.

The type restrictions on the formal parameters of functions and type generators determine a distinction between well-typed and ill-formed expressions. The Ontic system will not invoke the definition of a function or type generator unless the arguments to the function or type generator have been proven to be of the correct type; the Ontic system effectively type-checks expressions before it expands definitions. Given the expressive power of the Ontic type system, however, one can easily show that there are well-typed expressions which fail to type check. In the Ontic system type checking involves theorem proving based on a lemma library. Many of the lemmas of the lemma library state that certain

```
(DEFTERM (POWER-SET (S SET))
  (THE-SET-OF-ALL (SUBSET-OF S)))

(DEFTYPE (LOWER-BOUND-OF
            (S (SUBSET-OF (U-SET P)))
            (P POSET))
  (LAMBDA ((X (MEMBER-OF (U-SET P))))
    (IS-EVERY (MEMBER-OF S)
              (GREATER-OR-EQUAL-TO X P))))

(DEFTYPE (GREATEST-LOWER-BOUND-OF
            (S (SUBSET-OF (U-SET P)))
            (P POSET))
  (LAMBDA ((X (LOWER-BOUND-OF S P)))
    (IS-EVERY (LOWER-BOUND-OF S P)
              (LESS-OR-EQUAL-TO X P))))

(DEFTYPE COMPLETE-LATTICE
  (LAMBDA ((P POSET))
    (FORALL ((S (SUBSET-OF (U-SET P))))
      (EXISTS-SOME (GREATEST-LOWER-BOUND-OF S P)))))
```

Figure 1.4
Some Ontic Definitions

objects have certain types; not surprisingly, such lemmas play an important role in determining if an expression is well typed. It is often the case that a given expression fails to type check using one lemma library but succeeds in type checking given a stronger lemma library.

1.2.5 Summary

In addition to providing a distinction between well-typed and ill-formed expressions, the Ontic type vocabulary seems to allow for concise and natural formal statements. For example the IS-EVERY phrase constructor allows the concise expression of statements that would normally require explicit quantification. Similarly, the EXISTS-SOME phrase constructor uses the type vocabulary to make concise existential statements. Types are also used by the phrase constructors THE-SET-OF-ALL, THE, and EXACTLY-ONE.

The definitions in figure 1.4 should provide an indication of the conciseness and expressive power of the Ontic language. Jonathan Rees
spent about a month defining various mathematical concepts in Ontic.
Starting with only the fundamental notions described above, he used
the Ontic language to formally define groups, rings, ideals in a ring,
fields, the natural numbers, the real numbers (defined both as a to-
tally ordered complete field and as Dedekind cuts), topological spaces,
continuous functions, homotopy of maps between topological spaces, the
fundamental group of a topological space, differentiable functions on the
reals, the derivative of a function, the notion of a category and products
and limits in arbitrary categories. The ease with which Rees expressed
these concepts suggests that any mathematical concept can be readily
expressed in Ontic.

1.3   Examples of Verification

Object-oriented inference operates in a context. A context consists of
three things: a lemma library, a set of focus objects and set of suppositions about the focus objects. Figure 1.5 gives a block diagram of the
object-oriented inference mechanisms used in the Ontic system. The inference process is forward chaining; it draws conclusions from the lemma
library without being given any goal formula. It is well known that unrestricted forward chaining from a large lemma library leads to an immediate combinatorial explosion — vast numbers of formulas are generated
where each formula can be derived from the given lemmas in only a few
steps. The forward chaining inference mechanisms used in the Ontic
system, however, are guided by the focus objects. The focus objects are
Ontic terms, expressions that denote objects. The system restricts its
inference process to formulas that are in some sense "about" the focus
objects. There are four basic inference mechanisms: Boolean constraint
propagation, congruence closure, focused binding (also called semantic
modulation), and automatic universal generalization. The first two inference mechanisms are well known inference procedures for the quantifier-
free predicate calculus with equality. The last two inference mechanisms
are unique to the Ontic system. These four inference mechanisms are
discussed in section 1.4 and are presented in detail in [MCAL87]. In a
given context the four forward chaining inference mechanisms generate

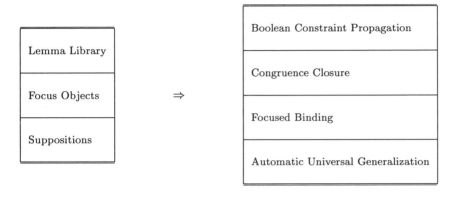

Figure 1.5
A Block Diagram of Object-Oriented Inference

a set of formulas about the focus objects called "obvious truths".

The Ontic system provides an interactive environment for developing and checking arguments. The result of an interaction with the system is a machine readable argument that establishes some lemma. The textual representation of a machine readable argument will be called an *argument expression*. When the Ontic system reads an argument expression it adds lemmas to the lemma library. Figure 1.6 shows the definition of a family of sets and the family intersection of a family of sets together with an argument expression which establishes that if F is a family of sets, and S is a set which is a subset of every member of F, then S is a subset of the intersection of all sets in F. The line numbers shown in figure 1.6 are for reference purposes only; they are not part of the argument expression. The argument expression shown in figure 1.6 is an IN-CONTEXT expres-

sion. An IN-CONTEXT expression always has two parts: a set of focus
objects and suppositions to be added to the current context, and a body
which consists of a list of argument expressions to be read in the context
which results from adding the new suppositions and focus objects. Lines
1 through 5 specify a context whose focus objects consist of a family of
sets F, an arbitrary set S, and the family intersection INT of the family
F and which has a single supposition consisting of the statement that
every member of F is a superset of S. Given the definitions of the terms
involved, and the supposition that every member of F is a superset of
S, it follows that S is a subset of INT. However the forward chaining
inference mechanisms are not strong enough to derive this fact in this
context. The interactive Ontic environment allows the user to enter a
context and ask questions about what has been derived in that context;
if the user enters the context specified in lines 1 through 5 and asks if
S is a subset of INT the system replies that it does not know. The user
can then provide a more detailed argument, given in lines 6 through 10,
which the Ontic system can verify. Argument expressions such as that
shown in 1.6 are generated during interactive sessions with the Ontic
system; the user need not be able to anticipate what the system will
derive in a given context.

The argument given in lines 6 through 10 of figure 1.6 is based on the
following reasoning: To show that the set S is a subset of INT we must
show that every member of S is a member of INT. To do this we can
consider some arbitrary member X of the set S. Before we can consider
a member of S, however, we must introduce the supposition that S is
non-empty. Any attempt to introduce a focus object of a type that is not
known to exist leads to an error. The suppositions and focus objects of
an IN-CONTEXT expression are added sequentially so that the focus object
of line 7 is introduced into a context in which the supposition of line 6 is
already present. Now consider the context specified by lines 1 through
5 together with lines 6 and 7 (but not 8). In this context there are four
focus objects and two suppositions. If the user enters this context and
asks the interactive Ontic system if X is a member of INT the system
answers that it does not know. At this point the user may be mystified
as to why the system does not "see" the obvious fact that X is indeed
a member of the family intersection INT. Before proceeding further, the
user may review the definition of the function FAMILY-INTERSECTION.
This definition states that X is a member of the family intersection just

```
(DEFTYPE FAMILY-OF-SETS
   (LAMBDA ((F NON-EMPTY-SET))
      (IS-EVERY (MEMBER-OF F) SET)))

(DEFTERM (FAMILY-INTERSECTION (F FAMILY-OF-SETS))
   (THE-SET-OF-ALL
      (LAMBDA ((X (MEMBER-OF-MEMBER-OF F)))
         (IS-EVERY (MEMBER-OF F) (SET-CONTAINING X)))))
```

```
1   (IN-CONTEXT ((LET-BE F FAMILY-OF-SETS)
2                (LET-BE S SET)
3                (SUPPOSE (IS-EVERY (MEMBER-OF F)
4                                  (SUPERSET-OF S)))
5                (LET-BE INT (FAMILY-INTERSECTION F)))
6      (IN-CONTEXT ((SUPPOSE (EXISTS (MEMBER-OF S)))
7                   (LET-BE X (MEMBER-OF S))
8                   (LET-BE S2 (MEMBER-OF F)))
9         (NOTE (IS S (SUBSET-OF INT))))
10     (NOTE (IS S (SUBSET-OF INT))))
```

Figure 1.6
An Argument Expression

in case X is a member of every set in the family F; to show that X is in INT we must show that X is in every member of F. To do this we consider an arbitrary member of F, i.e. we introduce another focus object, S2, which is an arbitrary member of F (families of sets are defined to be non-empty so the system knows that such a member exists).

Now consider the context specified by lines 1 though 8. In this context the forward chaining inference mechanisms automatically derive the fact that X is a member of S2. Furthermore, since S2 is an arbitrary member of F, the system uses automatic universal generalization to derive the fact that every member of F contains X. But this implies that X is a member of the family intersection INT. Finally, since X is an arbitrary member of S, the system derives the fact that S is a subset of INT. Thus, in the context specified by lines 1 through 8, the forward chaining inference mechanisms deduce that S is a subset of INT.

Line 9 of the argument expression of figure 1.6 is a NOTE expression. In

general, every argument expression is either an `IN-CONTEXT` expression
or a `NOTE` expression. When the Ontic system reads a `NOTE` expressions
it adds a lemma to its lemma library. The `NOTE` expression on line 9
causes the following lemma to be added to the lemma library:

```
(FORALL ((F FAMILY-OF-SETS)
         (S SET))
   (=> (AND (IS-EVERY (MEMBER-OF F) (SUPERSET-OF S))
            (EXISTS-SOME (MEMBER-OF S)))
       (IS S (SUBSET-OF (FAMILY-INTERSECTION F)))))
```

In general, when the system reads a note expression it constructs the
universal closure of the implication which states that the suppositions
active in the current context imply the noted formula. This universal
closure is then added to the lemma library. The above lemma is not the
desired result however; the above lemma only handles the case where S
is non-empty. To handle the general case the user returns to the context
specified by lines 1 through 5 of figure 1.6.

The lemma generated by lines 6 through 9 states that the result holds
in the case where S is non-empty. Given this lemma a simple `NOTE` expression on line 10 finishes the argument. When the system reads the
`NOTE` expression on line 10 it performs a refutation proof. The lemma

```
(IN-CONTEXT ((LET-BE F FAMILY-OF-SETS)
             (LET-BE S SET)
             (SUPPOSE (IS-EVERY (MEMBER-OF F)
                                (SUPERSET-OF S)))
             (LET-BE INT (FAMILY-INTERSECTION F))
             (PUSH-GOAL (IS S (SUBSET-OF INT))))

  (IN-CONTEXT ((SUPPOSE (EXISTS (MEMBER-OF S)))
              (LET-BE X (MEMBER-OF S))
              (LET-BE S2 (MEMBER-OF F)))
    (NOTE-GOAL))

  (NOTE-GOAL))
```

Figure 1.7
Goals as a textual convenience

generated by lines 6 though 9 is not sufficient to cause the forward chaining inference mechanisms to generate the statement that S is a subset
of INT in the context specified by lines 1 through 5. However, when
the system reads a NOTE expression where the formula being noted has
not been proven by forward chaining it automatically constructs a new
context which contains the supposition that the assertion to be noted is
false. In the case of the note expression on line 10, the forward chaining
inference mechanisms use the lemma generated by lines 6 through 9 to
generate a contradiction in the context containing the supposition that
S is not a subset of INT. Thus the formula to be noted is established by
refuting its negation. As a result of reading the NOTE expression on line
10 the system adds the following formula to its lemma library:

```
(FORALL ((F FAMILY-OF-SETS)
         (S SET))
  (=> (IS-EVERY (MEMBER-OF F) (SUPERSET-OF S))
      (IS S (SUBSET-OF (FAMILY-INTERSECTION F)))))
```

The two NOTE expressions in figure 1.6 correspond to a case analysis.
The first NOTE expression handles the case where S is non-empty. The
second NOTE expression handles the case where S is empty. In general,
multiple NOTE expressions for the same statement correspond to a case
analysis. Often, as in this example, the context for the last case does
not need to be explicitly constructed because an automatic refutation
process initiated by the last NOTE expression effectively constructs the
context for the last case.

When several NOTE expressions involve the same noted assertion one
can introduce a "goal" into a context and use (NOTE-GOAL) rather than
NOTE. In general a context is associated with a stack of goals and the
expression (NOTE-GOAL) is simply an abbreviation for noting the latest
goal on the stack. The presence of goals in a context has no effect on the
inference mechanisms. Using goals the argument expression of figure 1.6
can be rewritten as shown in figure 1.7.

The Ontic interpreter is able to use a large lemma library without
human assistance — the system automatically applies facts from the
lemma library whenever it enters a new context. Figure 1.8 shows the
lemma established by the argument expression of figure 1.6 together
with two other facts. The first fact states that for every family of sets

```
(FORALL ((F FAMILY-OF-SETS)
         (S SET))
    (=> (IS-EVERY (MEMBER-OF F)
                  (SUPERSET-OF S))
        (IS S (SUBSET-OF (FAMILY-INTERSECTION F)))))

(FORALL ((F FAMILY-OF-SETS)
         (S (MEMBER-OF F)))
    (IS (FAMILY-INTERSECTION F)
        (SUBSET-OF S)))

(FORALL ((S1 SET)
         (S2 SET))
    (=> (AND (IS S1 (SUBSET-OF S2))
             (IS S2 (SUBSET-OF S1)))
        (= S1 S2)))
```

Figure 1.8
Some Simple Facts

F, every member of F contains (as a subset) the family intersection of F. The second states that, for two sets, if each is a subset of the other, then the two sets are equal. Figure 1.9 is a proof which makes use of the facts in figure 1.8. We assume that the lemmas in figure 1.8 have been placed in the lemma library and are therefore available to the Ontic interpreter. The argument in figure 1.9 goes as follows: Let S be any set and let S2 be any subset of S. Let F be the set of all subsets of S which contain the set S2. We wish to show that the family intersection of F equals the set S2. First the user focuses on the family intersection of F by abbreviating this intersection with the symbol INT. Next the user focuses on an arbitrary member of the family F. Focusing on arbitrary member of F causes the system to "realize" various facts about F. For example every member of F is a set and thus F is a family of sets. By proving that F is a family of sets the system establishes that the term (FAMILY-INTERSECTION F) is well typed and thus the definition of FAMILY-INTERSECTION can be invoked. Furthermore S3 is a superset of S2 so S2 is a subset of S3 and by universal generalization S2 is a subset of every member of F. Once the system deduces that F is a family of sets and every member of F is a

```
(IN-CONTEXT ((LET-BE S SET)
             (LET-BE S2 (SUBSET-OF S))
             (LET-BE F (THE-SET-OF-ALL
                         (AND-TYPE (SUBSET-OF S)
                                   (SUPERSET-OF S2)))))
  (IN-CONTEXT ((PUSH-GOAL (= S2 (FAMILY-INTERSECTION F))))
    (IN-CONTEXT ((LET-BE INT (FAMILY-INTERSECTION F))
                 (LET-BE S3 (MEMBER-OF F)))
      (NOTE-GOAL))))
```

Figure 1.9
A Proof Using Lemmas

set which contains S2 the system automatically applies the first lemma
in figure 1.8 and realizes that S2 is a subset of the intersection INT.
The system also realizes that the set S2 is a member of the family F
and applies the the second lemma in figure 1.8 thus realizing that the
intersection INT is a subset of S2. Finally the system applies the the
third fact in figure 1.8 and realizes that INT equals S2.

The Ontic interpreter makes no distinction between definitions and
lemmas; definitions are just universally quantified equations which are
accessed in the same manner as lemmas. The proof shown in figure 1.9
relies on definitions as well as the lemmas shown in figure 1.8. The proof
shown in figure 1.8 does not involve any previously proven lemmas but
it does involve the definition of the intersection of a family of sets.

In general, the user need not make explicit references to definitions
and lemmas. The user relies on the system to use definitions and lemmas whenever they are appropriate. For example, consider an arbitrary
lemma of the form (FORALL ((x τ_1) (y τ_2)) $\Phi(x, y)$). This "lemma"
might actually be a definition in which case Φ is an equation. The Ontic
system will automatically use this lemma in any context where there are
two focus objects A and B such that A is an instance of τ_1 and B is an
instance of τ_2. In general, a universally quantified lemma such as the one
shown above will be instantiated with all combinations of focus objects
that match the type restrictions of the lemma. Once the lemmas have
been instantiated with the focus objects, the system applies the forward
chaining inference techniques of Boolean constraint propagation, congruence closure, and automatic universal generalization. The instantiation

process that invokes facts from the lemma library is a graph-theoretic marker-propagation inheritance mechanism called *focused binding* or *semantic modulation*. The focused binding mechanism achieves the effect of instantiation but avoids constructing the formulas that normally result from syntactic substitution.

One way of measuring the performance of a verification system is to compare the length of a natural argument with the length of a corresponding machine readable proof. The ratio of the length of a machine readable proof to the length of the corresponding natural argument is called the *expansion factor* for that proof. Figure 1.10 shows both an English natural argument (taken from a textbook on lattice theory, [GRAT78] page 24) and a corresponding Ontic proof. The natural argument contains 75 words and mathematical symbols, while the Ontic proof contains 73 symbols, yielding a word count expansion factor of about one. For the most part the "clear and necessary" steps of this particular natural argument correspond to statements that the Ontic interpreter can verify in a single step.

The natural argument shown in figure 1.10 concerns complete lattices. A complete lattice is a partially ordered set P such that every subset of P has both a least upper bound and a greatest lower bound. The argument in figure 1.10 shows that if every subset of a partially ordered set P has a least upper bound, then every subset of P must also have a greatest lower bound. In the argument from Gratzer's book, shown in figure 1.10, the least upper bound of a set H is denoted $\bigvee H$ and the greatest lower bound of H is denoted $\bigwedge H$. In the Ontic proof the goals are numbered so that one can more easily see the association between the statement of the goal and the achievement of the goal.

A different measure of the length of an argument is obtained by counting the number of type expressions rather than words. The number of type expressions used in an argument provides a rough measure of the number of "statements" involved. A direct translation of the natural argument in figure 1.10 into Ontic would contain 14 type expressions while the actual Ontic proof contains only 13 type expressions yielding an expansion factor of about one. Thus the basic result that the Ontic proof is about the same length as the English proof does not depend on the particular way in which one measures length.

In checking the proof in figure 1.10 the Ontic interpreter makes use of a large lemma library. The system uses some basic facts about partial

Proof. Let P be a poset in which $\bigvee S$ exists for all $S \subseteq P$. For $H \subseteq P$, let K be the set of all lower bounds of H. By hypothesis $\bigvee K$ exists; set $a = \bigvee K$. If $h \in H$, then $h \geq k$ for all $k \in K$; therefore $h \geq a$ and $a \in K$. Thus a is the greatest member of K, that is $a = \bigwedge H$.

```
(IN-CONTEXT ((LET-BE P POSET)
             (SUPPOSE (FORALL ((S (SUBSET-OF (U-SET P))))
                          (EXISTS (LEAST-UPPER-BOUND-OF S P))))
             (LET-BE H (SUBSET-OF (U-SET P)))
             (PUSH-GOAL
               (EXISTS (GREATEST-LOWER-BOUND-OF H P)))); #1
  (IN-CONTEXT
      ((LET-BE K (THE-SET-OF-ALL (LOWER-BOUND-OF H P)))
       (LET-BE a (THE (LEAST-UPPER-BOUND-OF K P))))
    (IN-CONTEXT ((PUSH-GOAL (IS a (LOWER-BOUND-OF H P)))); #2
      (IN-CONTEXT ((SUPPOSE (EXISTS (MEMBER-OF H)))
                   (LET-BE h0 (MEMBER-OF H)))
        (IN-CONTEXT
            ((PUSH-GOAL (IS h0 (UPPER-BOUND-OF K P)))); #3
          (IN-CONTEXT
                ((SUPPOSE (EXISTS (MEMBER-OF K)))
                 (LET-BE k0 (MEMBER-OF K)))
            (NOTE-GOAL)); #3
          (NOTE-GOAL))); #3
      (NOTE-GOAL)); #2
    (NOTE-GOAL))); #1
```

Figure 1.10
Least upper bounds yield greatest lower bounds.

orders together with the following facts:

1. The definitions of the concepts involved, e.g. the definition of partial orders, lower bound, least member and greatest lower bound.

2. The fact that if s is a subset of a partially ordered set p then the set of all lower bounds of s is a subset of p.

3. The fact that for any subset s of a partially ordered set p, there is

at most one least upper bound of s.

One can argue that the expansion factor measured for the proof of figure 1.10 is too low because the Ontic interpreter was allowed to use pre-proven lemmas that are not shown in the formal proof. But all of the lemmas used by the Ontic interpreter in proving this theorem are of general interest and have in fact been used in several different contexts. Furthermore the last two lemmas listed above have simple one or two line proofs in the Ontic system and thus if those lemmas had not been in the lemma library the proof shown in figure 1.10 would not be much longer.

It seems likely that human mathematicians unconsciously invoke a large data base of general facts when they think about mathematical objects. Furthermore, it seems likely that in familiarizing oneself with a new domain one must verify a large body of "trivial" facts and incorporate these facts into the way one thinks about the domain.

Bell and Machover's text on mathematical logic gives a more concise proof of the lemma of figure 1.10 ([BELL77] page 127). In the proof a least upper bound is called a supremum and a greatest lower bound is called an infimum.

> Let L be a partially ordered set in which each subset has
> a supremum. Let X be a subset of L, and let Y be the set
> of lower bounds of X in L. Then Y has a supremum z and
> it is not hard to see that z is the infimum of X.

A direct translation of the statements in Bell and Machover's into the language Ontic would contain 7 type expressions while the machine verifiable Ontic proof has 13 type expressions yielding a predicate count expansion factor of about two. While Bell and Machover's proof is clearly shorter than Gratzer's proof, Bell and Machover's proof includes the phrase "and it is not hard to see that". This phrase seems to be an admission that the given proof is not complete. Gratzer's proof, on the other hand, contains no such phrase and we must take Gratzer's proof as a fully expanded (complete) proof.

A complete listing of a mathematical development that ends with a proof of the Stone representation theorem for Boolean lattices is presented in [MCAL87]. This development provides a large number of examples of Ontic proofs and these proofs can be used to evaluate the Ontic

Lemma	Predicate Count Expansion Factor	Word Count Expansion Factor
If arbitrary least upper bounds exist then arbitrary greatest lower bounds also exist.	.9	1.0
Every filter is contained in an ultrafilter.	1.3	1.2
If F is an ultrafilter and $x \vee y \in F$ then $x \in F$ or $y \in F$.	2.1	2.7
Every Boolean algebra is isomorphic to a field of sets.	2.0	1.7

Table 1.1
Various Measurements of the Expansion Factor

verifier. Table 1.1 shows four expansion factor measurements taken from four of the larger proofs done in the Ontic system. The table lists both a predicate count expansion factor and a word count expansion factor for each test case. Both the natural argument and the corresponding Ontic proofs for each test case can be found in [MCAL87].

The machine readable proofs underlying table 1.1 relied on an extensive lemma library and the expansion factor measurements are thus open to the criticism that parts of the machine readable proof have been hidden in the lemma library. However, once a sufficiently large lemma library has been constructed, it should be possible to prove new theorems without extending the basic lemma library. I believe that the numbers listed in table 1.1 are accurate in that, with a mature lemma library, new theorems can be verified with small expansion factors even if the expansion factor takes into account all lemmas added during the verification.

1.4   The Inference Mechanisms

All of the inference mechanisms used in the Ontic system manipulate labelings of a graph structure. More specifically, the Ontic system compiles the lemma library into a graph structure where the nodes in the graph structure correspond to unique expressions in the formal language. There are nodes that correspond to terms, formulas, type expressions, function expressions and type generator expressions. The graph structure has nine different kinds of "links" where each link expresses a certain way that nodes are related. For example if n is the node corresponding to the type expression (LOWER-BOUND-OF s p) then there is a subexpression link that relates n to the three nodes that correspond to the expressions LOWER-BOUND-OF, s and p. There are also links that express Boolean constraints among formula nodes, links that relate a lambda function to the node representing the bound variable and the body of that expression, and six other kinds of links.

A labeling of the graph structure consists of two parts: a partial truth labeling on formula nodes, and a color labeling on all nodes. For each formula node p the partial truth labeling either assigns p the label *true*, assigns p the label *false*, or leaves p unlabeled. The color nodes represent an equivalence relation on nodes: two nodes with the same color label are considered to be equivalent, i.e. proven equal in the current context. Whenever an inference is made the system updates the labeling: either a formula is assigned a truth label or two equivalence classes are merged by recoloring one class to be the same color as the other class. Any such inference process for updating labels on a fixed graph structure must terminate because there are only finitely many formula nodes that can be assigned truth labels and every merger of equivalence classes reduces the number of equivalence classes remaining.

The same underlying graph structure can be used in many different contexts. Graph structure is never thrown away: each time new graph structure is created it is saved for use in other contexts. Truth and color labels, on the other hand, are temporary; they are thrown away, for example, when the system stops considering a particular supposition or focus object.

This section presents an informal discussion of the inference mechanisms which operate on the graph structure and the way in which the graph structure is constructed from the lemma library. A precise description of the Ontic language, the inference rules used with Ontic, and the implemented inference mechanisms is given in chapters 4, 5, and 6.

1.4.1 Inference for Quantifier-Free Logic

The Boolean constraint propagation and congruence closure algorithms were originally designed as inference mechanisms for quantifier-free logic. Boolean constraint propagation adds truth labels in response to Boolean constraints and previous truth labels. For example, if the node for the implication (=> Φ Ψ) is labeled true, and the node for Φ is labeled true, then Boolean constraint propagation will ensure that the node for Ψ is labeled true. Similarly, if the node for (=> Φ Ψ) is labeled true, and the node Ψ is labeled false, then Boolean constraint propagation will ensure that the node for Φ is labeled false.

Boolean constraint propagation is also responsible for ensuring a certain relationship between color labels and the truth labels of nodes representing equalities. To ensure this relationship the system may merge equivalence classes in response to the addition of a truth label or, alternatively, add a truth label in response to the merger of equivalence classes. More specifically, let p be a node which represents an equation between the expressions represented by nodes n_1 and n_2. If the equality node p is assigned the label *true* then the system ensures that nodes n_1 and n_2 have the same color label, i.e. are in the same equivalence class. On the other hand if the nodes n_1 and n_2 are in the same equivalence class then the system ensures that p is assigned the label *true*.[7]

Congruence closure is responsible for ensuring that the equivalence relation represented by the color labels respects the substitution of equals for equals. For example, consider the expressions (POWER-SET s_1) and (POWER-SET s_2). Congruence closure ensures that if the nodes representing the terms s_1 and s_2 have the same color label (are in the same equivalence class) then the nodes representing (POWER-SET s_1) and (POWER-SET s_2) also have the same color label. When two equivalence classes are merged congruence closure may merge additional equivalence classes in order to ensure that the equivalence relation respects the substitution of equals for equals.

---

[7]If n_1 and n_2 are in the same equivalence class and the equality node p has been labeled false by some other inference process then the system signals a contradiction.

1.4.2   Focused Binding

Recall that a context consists of a lemma library, a set of focus objects
and a set of suppositions about the focus objects. Focused binding is
a way of applying the universally quantified formulas in the lemma library to the focus objects in a context. This is done using an inheritance
mechanism similar in spirit to Fahlman's virtual copy mechanism based
on marker propagation [FHLM79]. More specifically, each type τ which
has been compiled into a node in the graph structure is associated with
a set of (typically two or three) *generic individuals* of that type. Information that is known to hold for a given type is explicitly stated about
the generic individuals of that type. A focus object which is known to
be an instance of type τ becomes a "virtual copy" of one of the generic
individuals of type τ and thus inherits information from that individual.

Each generic individual is a term node in the graph structure. Information which is known to hold for the type τ is explicitly stated about
each generic individual of type τ. More specifically, if the system compiles the formula (FORALL ($(x\ \tau)$) $\Phi(x)$) into graph structure then for
each generic individual g of type τ which is added to the graph structure,
the system constructs a Boolean constraint equivalent to the following
implication.

```
(=> (AND (FORALL ((x τ)) Φ(x))
         (EXISTS-SOME τ))

    Φ(g))
```

Given the above constraint, if the universally quantified formula is true
in a context, and instances of type τ are known to exist in that context,
then the body of the universal formula is known to be true for each
generic individual of type τ. In this way everything that is known about
the type in general is explicitly stated about the generic individuals of
that type.

The classification process assigns types to focus objects. Classification
is needed in order for focus objects to inherit information from generic
individuals. The system classifies a focus object r by collecting a set,
types(r), of types known to hold for r according to the following rules:

  1. If the node for the formula (IS r τ) is labeled true then τ is

included in *types(r)*.

2. If s is a term that is in the same equivalence class as the focus object r, and if the formula (IS s σ) is labeled true, then σ is included in *types(r)*.

3. If τ is a member of *types(r)*, and the formula (IS-EVERY τ σ) is labeled true, then σ is included in *types(r)*.

4. If τ is a member of *types(r)* and σ is a type in the same equivalence class (with the same color as) τ then σ is included in *types(r)*.

Focused binding causes a given focus object to inherit information from a given generic individual. More specifically, for each focus object r and each type τ in the set *types(r)* the system chooses a generic individual g of type τ and constructs the binding $g \mapsto r$. The generic individual g can be thought of as a typed variable and the binding $g \mapsto r$ can be thought of as a variable binding. In the Ontic system the variable binding $g \mapsto r$ is implemented via the color labels: when the system constructs the binding $g \mapsto r$ it assigns g and r the same color label, thereby making g equivalent to r. When g is made equivalent to r, the congruence closure mechanism is used to "unify" or "match" the expressions involving the generic individual g with the expressions involving the focus object r. In this way the focus object r becomes a virtual copy of the generic individual g. Since general knowledge about the type τ is explicitly stated about the generic individual g, general knowledge about the type τ becomes effectively stated about the focus object r. In this way general facts in the lemma library are effectively applied to focus objects of the correct type.

The focused binding process is sometimes called *semantic modulation* because it involves modulating (changing) the interpretation of a fixed generic individual. The same generic individual can be bound to different focus objects in different contexts. In this way the system modulates the semantic denotation of the generic individual, hence the term semantic modulation.

1.4.3 Automatic Universal Generalization

The fourth inference mechanism used by the Ontic system is automatic universal generalization. Universal generalization can be applied when the system has deduced a fact about an arbitrary individual and no assumptions have been made about that individual. More specifically, a universal generalization inference can be made if:

- g is a generic individual of type τ.

- The system has labeled the node for a formula $\Phi(g)$ true.

- No assumptions have been made about the individual g other than the assumption that it is an instance of type τ.

- No free variable of $\Phi(g)$ has a type that depends on g. The notion of dependence used here is the same as that defined above: τ depends on x just in case x appears free in τ or some free variable of τ has a type which depends on x.

When the above conditions are met the system can infer the universal closure (FORALL ((x τ)) $\Phi(x)$).

There are several things to note about automatic universal generalization. First, this inference mechanism does not construct new formulas or new graph structure; automatic universal generalization is only applied when the graph already contains nodes for the formulas $\Phi(g)$ and the universal closure (FORALL ((x τ)) $\Phi(x)$). Second, types play a central role in the automatic universal generalization mechanism. When the system proves the formula $\Phi(g)$, where g is a generic individual of type τ, the resulting universal statement applies to all instances of τ. Third, without the last restriction universal generalization is unsound. For example, consider a generic individual y that ranges over numbers greater than the generic number x. Without making any assumptions about x and y other than that they are both instances of their respective types, the system can deduce that x is less than y. It does not follow, however, that all numbers are less than y; there is no largest number. The fact that x is less than y does not imply that all numbers are less then y because the x "occurs in" y; x is a free variable in the type of y. The same proof that shows that the Ontic occurs-check procedure is sound for focused binding can be used to show that the Ontic occurs-check procedure leads to sound universal generalization.

The above notion of universal generalization can be made more powerful by relaxing the restriction that no assumptions have been made about the arbitrary individual being generalized over. More specifically one can perform universal generalization under the following conditions:

- g is a generic individual of type τ.

- The system has labeled the node for a formula $\Phi(g)$ true.

- The system has bound g via the binding $g \mapsto h$.

- h is a generic individual of type σ where σ has the same color label as τ in the current context.

- No assumptions have been made about h.

- h does not "occur in" any free variable of $\Phi(g)$ other than g.

When the above conditions are met the system can infer the universal closure (**FORALL** $((x\ \tau))\ \Phi(x)$).

Again, note that this inference mechanism does not construct new formulas or add new graph structure. In order for this inference mechanism to be applied, all of the formulas involved must already be compiled into nodes in the graph structure.

To see the importance of the more general automatic universal generalization mechanism, consider a subset s of a partially ordered set p and the set u of all lower bounds of s as a subset of p. Now consider a member x of s. By definition, u is the set of lower bounds of s so x is an upper bound of u. It turns out that in the Ontic system proving this last statement requires universal generalization. More specifically, the Ontic system must focus on an arbitrary member y of u and note that x is greater than or equal to y. Since y is an arbitrary member of u, and x is greater than or equal to y, x must be greater than or equal to all members of u. In this situation the system will construct the bindings $s' \mapsto u$ and $z \mapsto y$. Here s' is a generic individual ranging over arbitrary subsets of p and z is a generic individual ranging over members of s'. Now y is a generic individual ranging over members of u and z is a generic individual ranging over members of s', so z and y are different generic individuals whose types happen to be equal in the current context. Furthermore z is bound to y. In this situation the system generalizes over the variable z rather than the variable y. The system must generalize over z rather than y because the definition of upper bound is stated about the generic subset s' rather than the particular subset u and thus the quantified formula in question quantifies over members of s' rather than members of u.

All of the inference mechanisms used in the Ontic system run concurrently and interact with each other. Inferences can lead to more knowledge about the types of focus objects; this can lead to more bindings, which can lead in turn to more inference. The time required to finish the overall inference process is bounded by the size of the graph structure. This is because the inference processes can only add as many truth labels as there are formula nodes and can only merge as many equivalence classes as there are nodes in total. The factors that contribute to the size of the graph structure are discussed below.

1.4.4   The Size of the Graph Structure

When a new focus object r of type τ is introduced, it is possible that all generic individuals of type τ have either already been bound to other objects or occur in the focus object r and thus cannot be bound to r. In this case the system creates a new generic individual of type τ and copies all of the information known about type τ as explicit statements about that new generic individual. Once the generic individual has been constructed, however, it is saved and can be used in other contexts. For most arguments there are already enough generic individuals in the graph structure to accommodate the focus objects and no new graph structure is created. However, if there are not enough generic individuals to accommodate the focus objects, then generic individuals are created on demand as focus objects are introduced. As generic individuals are created the underlying graph structure expands.

The size of the graph structure created by the Ontic compiler is determined by the library of mathematical facts and by the number of generic individuals that have been created for each type. Fortunately, for any given bound on the level of quantifier nesting, the size of the graph structure is linear in the size of the lemma library; the amount of graph structure is the sum over all lemmas of the amount of structure created by each lemma. This fact allows the Ontic system to be used with large libraries of mathematical facts. However, the cost of an individual lemma can be quite high. Consider a universally quantified lemma (FORALL ((x τ_1) (y τ_2) (z τ_3)) $\Phi(x,y,z)$). The body of this lemma will be copied for each triple g_1, g_2, g_3 where g_1, g_2 and

g_3 are generic individuals of type τ_1, τ_2 and τ_3 respectively. In general every quantified formula which is compiled into graph structure gets instantiated with every generic individual of the appropriate type. The number of copies of the body of the above lemma is $|\tau_1| \cdot |\tau_2| \cdot |\tau_3|$ where $|\tau_1|$, $|\tau_2|$ and $|\tau_3|$ are the numbers of generic individuals for τ_1, τ_2, and τ_3 respectively. Generic individuals are created on demand as new focus objects are introduced. If no more than n focus objects have been introduced in any one context then there will be at most n generic individuals of each type. If the maximum number of quantifiers used in any lemma is d then there can be no more than n^d copies of the body of each lemma. Lemmas rarely involve more than three quantifiers and most sessions with the Ontic interpreter involve at most five simultaneous focus objects. Thus a typical lemma in a typical session generates no more than 5^3 or 125 instantiations. In practice this number is smaller because most lemmas quantify over highly specialized types and there are typically only a small number of generic individuals of specialized types. Again note that the size of the graph structure is *linear* in the size of the lemma library; the total amount of graph structure is just the sum over all lemmas of the amount of structure generated by each lemma. However, the size of graph structure is very sensitive to the maximum number of focus objects introduced in a given context. A good rule of thumb seems to be that the size of the graph structure is proportional to $n^3 |\Sigma|$ where n is the maximum number of focus objects introduced in any one context and $|\Sigma|$ is the size of the lemma library.

2 Comparison with Other Work

The Ontic system represents a synthesis of ideas from artificial intelligence and automated theorem proving. Constraint propagation is a forward chaining inference technique that terminates quickly because it monotonically fills a finite set of "slots"; the Ontic system monotonically generates truth and color labels for nodes in a finite graph structure. Congruence closure is a powerful theorem proving technique for reasoning about equality. Congruence closure is usually viewed as an inference procedure reasoning about equalities involving ground (variable-free) expressions. In the Ontic system, however, congruence closure is used as an integral part of general first-order theorem proving. Focused binding, also known as semantic modulation, is closely related to inheritance mechanisms which have been developed for knowledge representation languages and object oriented computer programming languages. Focused binding integrates inheritance with other theorem proving mechanisms. Congruence closure is used to implement a strong virtual copy mechanism that allows focus objects to inherit from generic individuals. Automatic universal generalization is perhaps the simplest and yet the most original feature of the Ontic system. Ontic brings all these ideas together in a single integrated inference process.

The first section of this chapter relates each of the four basic inference mechanisms used in Ontic with previous work in knowledge representation and automated theorem proving. The second section of the chapter relates Ontic's focused binding mechanism to unification. Focused binding and unification provide different ways of selecting and applying facts from a fact library. The third section of the chapter lists various theorem proving mechanisms other than those used in the Ontic system and attempts to show how they are related to Ontic. The final section of the chapter lists some of the general issues to be considered in constructing a proof verification system and discusses how Ontic and various other systems have addressed those issues.

2.1 Previous Ontic-Like Mechanisms

The following four sections discuss each of Ontic's four inference mechanisms in turn. The first three inference mechanisms are related to well known inference techniques. Ontic, however, brings these mechanisms together in an integrated, object oriented theorem proving process.

2.1.1 Constraint Propagation

There are many mechanisms in the artificial intelligence literature which
could be described as constraint propagators. By "constraint propagation" I mean an inference process whose running time, or number of
processing steps, is directly bounded by the size of a finite *constraint
network*. Ontic is a constraint propagation system in two ways. First
of all, one of the fundamental inference mechanisms is Boolean constraint propagation which is a special case of the arc-consistency constraint propagation technique for general constraint satisfaction problems [MACK77]. Second, all of Ontic's inference mechanisms operate
by labeling a graph structure. The graph structure is analogous to a
constraint network in that the total number of labeling operations is
directly bounded by the size of that graph structure.

Many artificial intelligence researchers have used constraint propagation. Waltz used constraint propagation to filter the possible interpretations of lines in a line drawings of polygonal physical objects [WLTZ75].
A line in a drawing of a scene can be interpreted as a convex edge on
single object, a concave edge on a single object or an edge between two
objects. A particular interpretation of an edge is called a "label" for that
edge. Vertices between edges provide constraints on the possible interpretations of edges. In Waltz line labeling a forward chaining inference
process systematically eliminates possible labelings of individual edges.
The running time of the process is directly bounded by the number of
edges and the number of labels that can be eliminated.

The Waltz line labeling procedure can be used in the more general setting of an arbitrary constraint satisfaction problem [MACK77]. A constraint satisfaction problem consists of a set of variables each of which
can be assigned one of a finite set of possible values and a set of constraints where each constraint restricts the simultaneous assignments for
a given subset of the variables. The arc-consistency procedure, which is
a straightforward generalization of Waltz labeling, systematically eliminates possible interpretations of variables based on local constraints.
The running time of the arc-consistency procedure is directly bounded
by the number of variables and the number of possible assignments for
each variable. Boolean constraint propagation is a special case of the
arc-consistency procedure where the variables are Boolean, i.e. they can
be assigned the labels *true* or *false*, and the constraints are disjunctive

clauses involving the Boolean variables.

Sussman and Steele have proposed a language for expressing constraints on real valued variables and constraint propagation techniques for dealing with such constraints [SUSS80]. The number of propagation operations performed by Sussman and Steele's system was directly bounded by the number of variables involved.

Nevins constructed a forward chaining geometry theorem prover which restricted the forward chaining inference process to an a priori fixed set of formulas [NEVN74]. Nevins' program used a diagram to focus the system's attention on certain lines. If a geometry problem has n points then there are $\binom{n}{2}$ possible line segments between these points. A diagram, however, specifies a subset of the $\binom{n}{2}$ lines, those actually drawn in the diagram. By limiting forward chaining to statements about these focused lines, the forward chaining process does not generate large numbers of irrelevant facts. With Nevins' focused forward chaining mechanism there is no need for the diagrammatic filter used by Gelernter [GLRT59].

Ontic's inference processes operate on a finite graph structure; the number of labeling operations is directly bounded by the size of that graph structure. The Ontic system can use the same graph structure in different contexts to reason about different focus objects. When a generic individual g is bound to a focus object r, a formula involving g can be viewed as a formula involving r; in the presence of bindings the formula nodes in the graph structure represent formulas about focus objects. Different bindings cause the nodes in the graph structure to represent statements about different objects.

2.1.2 Congruence Closure

Congruence closure is the process of "closing" an equivalence relation on expressions under the inference rule of substitution of equals for equals. Congruence closure was first discussed by Kozen for reasoning about finitely presented algebras [KOZN77]. Congruence closure has also been used by Nelson and Oppen in constructing fast decision procedures for a variety of problems that arise in automatic program verification [NELS80]. The congruence closure procedure used in the Ontic system is based on the procedure given by Downey, Sethi and Tarjan [DWNY80].

Ontic uses congruence closure both as a mechanism for reasoning about equality and as a replacement for unification. The relationship between Ontic's use of congruence closure and traditional unification is discussed in section 2.2.

2.1.3   Focused Binding as Inheritance

Focused binding can be viewed as an inheritance mechanism: information about a type is inherited by instances of that type. Type hierarchies and inheritance are also important in object oriented programming languages such as Smalltalk [INGS76]. In object-oriented programming, data types are organized into a hierarchy where one data type can be a subtype of another. Data objects are usually records with data fields. A given data object inherits both data fields and functional behavior from all the supertypes of its immediate type. A fairly rigorous, though not very general, treatment of some basic ideas in object-oriented programming is given in [CARD84].

Type hierarchies and inheritance also play a central role in many knowledge representation systems and object oriented programming languages. Frame-based knowledge representation languages typically allow the user to define "concepts" which he or she organizes into an "is-a" hierarchy (e.g. [BRAC85]). A concept represents a class of structured objects; the concept is associated with a set of "slots"; an instance of that concept is an object with specific "fillers" or "values" for the slots of the concept. For example, the concept *room* might have slots *ceiling*, *floor*, *walls*, and *furniture*. Any particular room will have a particular ceiling, a particular floor, and a particular set of pieces of furniture. Furthermore, a concept can place certain constraints on the slot fillers. For example, the concept *room* might specify that the furniture slot is always filled with a set of physical objects. The user could introduce the concept *auditorium* as a specialization of the concept *room* and the concept *auditorium* would then automatically "inherit" the slots and constraints of the concept *room*.

Ontic's focused binding mechanism is very similar to Fahlman's virtual copy mechanism based on marker propagation [FHLM79]. Fahlman proposed a semantic network formalism in which objects inherit information from classes by passing markers along links in the network. The marker passing is done in such a way that the object being considered becomes a "virtual copy" of generic objects which contain information about classes. In the Ontic system color labels are used instead of Fahlman's markers. A focus object is made into a virtual copy of a generic individual by assigning the generic individual the same color label as the focus object; congruence closure ensures that if two nodes have the same color label then they have identical properties.

In the Ontic system inheritance is just one aspect of an integrated theorem proving mechanism. Generic individuals are viewed as logical variables that range over a given type. Inheritance occurs when a generic individual g is bound to a focus object r via a binding $g \mapsto r$. Fahlman's inheritance mechanism, on the other hand, was not viewed as a formal inference mechanism and Fahlman did not propose integrating his inheritance mechanism with other formal inference techniques such as Boolean constraint propagation, congruence closure, or automatic universal generalization.

2.1.4 Automatic Universal Generalization

Automatic universal generalization arises from a very simple idea: if a fact is proven about a generic individual g of type τ and no assumptions have been made about g other than that g is an instance of τ, then the fact holds for all instances of τ. In spite of the simplicity of the underlying idea, Ontic's universal generalization technique seems to be unlike any previous automatic inference mechanism. For example, a comparison of Ontic and resolution theorem provers shows that when Ontic performs universal generalization it is treating a generic individual as a Skolem constant introduced by a universally quantified goal formula. But, unlike resolution, the Ontic system does not make any distinction between variables and Skolem constants. Generic individuals in Ontic are used in three different ways. If instances of a type τ are known to exist then each generic individual of type τ is asserted to be an instance of τ. In this way the generic individuals can be used as Skolem constants introduced by the premise that instances of τ exist. But generic individuals are also used as variables that can be bound to specific terms in much the same way that resolution variables are bound during unification. Generic individuals are used in yet a third way by the universal generalization mechanism; universal generalization treats generic individuals as Skolem constants introduced by universally quantified goal statements.

The real novelty of the Ontic system lies in the way that the above four inference mechanisms are brought together. Ontic integrates constraint propagation, congruence closure, inheritance, and universal generalization in a single labeling process on a fixed graph structure.

2.2   Unification Versus Focused Binding

One of the most striking features of the Ontic system, as compared to other theorem proving systems, is that Ontic does not use unification. Unification is often used to access information in a data base. A Prolog interpreter, for example, takes a goal formula and finds a production in the data base whose left hand side unifies with the given goal. A rewrite system takes an expression to be simplified and finds a rewrite rule in the data base whose left hand side unifies with the expression to be simplified. Under the set-of-support heuristic a resolution theorem prover finds a clause in the data base such that a literal of that clause unifies with a subgoal in the current problem. In all these cases the system is finding an expression in the data base which unifies with an expression in the current problem.

Ontic accesses information in the lemma library via the focused binding mechanism. Both unification and focused binding generate variable bindings which are useful to produce specialized instances of the general formulas in a data base. However, unification and focused binding generate variable bindings in very different ways. Unification starts with the expressions to be matched and generates variable bindings which lead to the match. Focused binding, on the other hand, starts with focus objects then generates variable bindings (bindings of generic individuals) and relies on congruence closure to generate "matches" between expressions involving variables and expressions involving the focus objects. Unification is a local process: unification is used in the application of a single rewrite rule or in a single resolution step. Focused binding, on the other hand, is a global process involving an arbitrary number of facts from the lemma library. Focused binding is integrated into the theorem-proving process. Automated inference and knowledge from the lemma library is used both in determining the types which apply to a given object and in determining equivalences between expressions after bindings have been performed.

Considerable research has been directed toward incorporating various kinds of knowledge (axiomatic theories) into unification. Equational axioms, such as the commutativity and associativity properties of addition, can be incorporated into the unification process so that, for example, $a + x$ matches $b + a$ with the binding $x \mapsto b$. Taxonomic information, information involving the classification of objects into types, can also be incorporated into the unification process. Because Ontic's focused binding mechanism is integrated with the theorem proving process, focused binding automatically incorporates both equational and taxonomic information into the matching process; any lemma in the lemma library may be used in Ontic's matching process. However, unlike most unification mechanisms, Ontic's matching process is not logically complete: it is possible that two expressions are provably equivalent and yet the Ontic system fails to match them. This is consistent with the overall design philosophy of the Ontic system; to ensure that the system always terminates quickly, completeness has been abandoned.

2.2.1 Unification Relative to Equational Theories

There has been a considerable amount of research dedicated to incorporating equational theories into unification. For example, consider addition as an associative and commutative operator. Now consider the problem of unifying $x + (a + b)$ and $a + (c + b)$. The binding $x \mapsto c$ unifies these two terms in the sense that the following equation holds for addition:

$$c + (a + b) = a + (c + b)$$

More generally, let Γ be a set of universally quantified equations between first order terms. For example, Γ might consist of the associative and commutative laws for addition. A general purpose theorem prover, such as a resolution system, could handle the equations in Γ simply by adding the equations in Γ to the data base of general facts. In practice, however, it seems more efficient to incorporate certain equational facts into the unification process. Once these facts have been incorporated into the unification process they can be removed from the general data base without loss of logical completeness.

A given set of equational axioms Γ has a corresponding unification problem. For any substitution σ and any expression u we define $\sigma(u)$ to be the result of simultaneously replacing all free variables in u with their image under σ. A *unification* of two expressions s and t relative to the axioms in Γ is a substitution σ which yields a match between s and

t relative to Γ, i.e. such that the equational formulas in Γ imply that $\sigma(s)$ equals $\sigma(t)$. If Γ states that $+$ is associative and commutative then the substitution $\{x \mapsto c\}$ unifies $x + (a + b)$ and $a + (c + b)$ relative to Γ. The unification problem for Γ is the problem of computing, for any given expressions s and t, a representation of all unifications of s and t relative to Γ.

If Γ consists of a single commutative operation then it is easy to determine if there exists a unification of any two given terms relative to Γ. On the other hand if Γ states that a binary operator $\times$ is associative, and $\times$ distributes over a binary operator $+$, then there is no procedure which can decide the existence of a unification of two arbitrary terms relative to Γ. These results and others are discussed in a review article by Siekmann [SIEK84].

It is interesting to compare unification relative to equational theories with Ontic's focused binding mechanism. Ontic's matching process (congruence closure) automatically incorporates equations from the lemma library. For example, suppose that Ontic's lemma library contains the associative and commutative laws for addition on the natural numbers shown in figure 2.1.

The first and second equations in figure 2.1 express the fact that addition is commutative and associative respectively. The third equation follows from the other two. If the third equation were not explicitly given, however, then when focusing on three generic numbers g_1, g_2 and g_3 the following equation would not be obvious to the Ontic system.

$$g_1 + (g_2 + g_3) = (g_2 + g_3) + g_1$$

To prove this equation in the absence of the third lemma, or to prove the third lemma from the other two, the system must focus on the sum $g_2 + g_3$ so that the commutative law is applied to $g_1 + (g_2 + g_3)$. The associative and commutative laws allow for twelve different ways of writing down the sum of g_1, g_2 and g_3: there are six different orders in which the numbers can appear and two different ways of parenthesizing each order. In the presence of the three lemmas given above all twelve ways of writing the sum are equivalent. The twelve nodes in the graph structure that represent the twelve different expressions for this sum are all in the same equivalence class; they have the same color label. Now suppose the user focuses on three particular numbers a, b and c. The

```
(FORALL ((X NATURAL-NUMBER)
         (Y NATURAL-NUMBER))
  (= (SUM-OF X Y)
     (SUM-OF Y X))))
(FORALL ((X NATURAL-NUMBER)
         (Y NATURAL-NUMBER)
         (Z NATURAL-NUMBER))
  (= (SUM-OF X (SUM-OF Y Z))
     (SUM-OF (SUM-OF X Y) Z)))
(FORALL ((X NATURAL-NUMBER)
         (Y NATURAL-NUMBER)
         (Z NATURAL-NUMBER))
  (= (SUM-OF X (SUM-OF Y Z))
     (SUM-OF (SUM-OF Y Z) X)))
```

Figure 2.1
Some Algebraic Laws

Ontic system will bind a generic number to each of these three particular numbers; assume that the system generates the bindings

$$g_1 \mapsto a$$

$$g_2 \mapsto b$$

$$g_3 \mapsto c$$

Given that all twelve expressions for the sum of g_1, g_2 and g_3 are in the same equivalence class, congruence closure together with the above bindings ensures that the term a+(b+c) is equivalent to the term b+(c+a). By using congruence closure as a matching mechanism, and by precompiling equational theories as equations involving generic individuals, the Ontic system automatically performs theory-relative matching. Unfortunately Ontic's matching process is not complete; the incompleteness is demonstrated by the need for the third lemma given above. On the other hand, as the example shows, one can always improve the power of the matching process by adding derived equational lemmas to the lemma library.

Ontic's focused binding mechanism automatically incorporates arbitrary equational lemmas into the congruence closure process; in the Ontic system one does not have to design a new theory-relative matching process for each new theory as one must do for theory relative unification. Ontic's mechanism has the disadvantage however that there is no guarantee of completeness — congruence closure may fail to equate semantically equal terms.

2.2.2 Unification Relative to Taxonomic Theories

Several researchers have studied unification relative to non-equational theories. Non-equational theories incorporated into the unification process are sometimes called *taxonomic theories* because they usually encode a classification of objects into types. The separation of "taxonomic" and "assertional" information has been discussed in the knowledge representation literature [BRAC82]. For example, consider the following axiom:

$$\forall x \, \mathbf{whale}(x) \Rightarrow \mathbf{mammal}(x)$$

This axiom expresses an inclusion relation between the "type" **whale** and the type **mammal**. Inclusion relations of this kind can be incorporated into the unification process and need not be stated explicitly in the data base of a general purpose theorem prover.

Walther has developed a unification algorithm that can incorporate any taxonomic theory expressible as a partial order on class symbols [WLT84a]. He showed that for any such taxonomic theory Γ and any two typed terms s and t the set of all unifications of s and t can be expressed with a finite set of most general unifiers (i.e. the unification problem is finitary). Furthermore he showed that if the type hierarchy is a tree then there is a single most general unifier.

Ait-Kaci and Nasr have given a unification algorithm for a more expressive class of taxonomic theories and propose using this algorithm in an implementation of the programming language PROLOG [AIT86]. Stickel has investigated the use of taxonomic theories in even greater generality although Stickel does not address unification as a mechanism for generating variable bindings (only the ground case is considered as lifting to the general case is "straightforward") [STIC85].

Inheritance via semantic modulation is based on taxonomic information. More specifically, the Ontic system classifies each focus object by associating each focus object with a set of types known to be true of that focus object. This classification process takes the type hierarchy into account. For example, if r is a focus object, σ is a type known to hold of r, and the formula (IS-EVERY σ τ) is labeled true, then the classification process will collect τ as a type known to hold of r.

Unlike unification, Ontic's focused binding mechanism integrates the use of taxonomic information with other theorem proving mechanisms. Ontic may prove a taxonomic theorem, i.e. a statement relating types, and use that statement immediately in classifying the current focus objects. Ontic's focused binding mechanism automatically incorporates arbitrary lemmas about the types of objects. There is no guarantee, however, that Ontic's focused binding mechanism will derive all the logical consequences of taxonomic information.

2.2.3 Higher-Order Unification

Unification has been generalized to allow for higher-order variables; higher-order unification can be used to bind variables that range over functions and predicates as well as variables ranging over first order terms. For example, consider the induction schema for Peano arithmetic.

$$P(0) \ \wedge \ \forall n \, (P(n) \Rightarrow P(n+1)) \ \Rightarrow \ \forall n \, P(n) \tag{2.1}$$

In this schema P is a variable which ranges over predicates. This schema can be instantiated with any predicate P and higher-order unification can be used to find bindings for P. For example, consider a function f which is known to be monotone:

$$\forall m \ \ f(m+1) \geq f(m) \tag{2.2}$$

and we wish to prove

$$\forall m \ \ f(m) \geq f(0) \tag{2.3}$$

To prove this last statement a backward chaining theorem prover might unify $P(n)$ from the conclusion of 2.1 with the goal $f(m) \geq f(0)$ from 2.3 yielding the bindings $n \mapsto m$ and $P \mapsto (\lambda(n) \, f(n) \geq f(0))$. A backward chaining inference system could then prove the antecedents of 2.1 under the above binding for the predicate P.

The first complete unification procedure for higher-order logic was constructed by Gerard Huet [HUET75]. Higher-order unification has been used effectively in at least two mathematical verification systems, Ketonen's EKL system [KTNN84] and Andrews' TPS [MILL82]. In both systems the higher-order unification procedure was found to terminate quickly in practice.

The Ontic system is higher-order in the same sense that axiomatic set theory is higher-order; functions and predicates can be "reified" as sets and thus first order variables can be made to range over functions and predicates. In the Ontic system the user can focus on a reified predicate Q and thus cause the system to bind variables to the predicate Q. This kind of "higher-order" binding was used many times in the proof of the Stone representation theorem.

While the Ontic system does allow for higher-order reasoning, the Ontic system does not adequately handle mathematical induction. Verifying induction proofs in the Ontic system results in a large expansion factor; the machine readable proofs are significantly longer than the natural language counterpart.

Higher-order unification provides one technique for reducing the expansion factor for induction proofs. The EKL system relies on higher order unification both in establishing the well formedness of recursive definitions and in performing induction arguments to prove properties of recursively defined functions. But there seem to be other, perhaps even better, techniques for reasoning about recursive definitions. The Boyer-Moore theorem prover is extremely effective in performing induction arguments but does not use higher order unification [BOYR79]. Ontic's weakness with regard to induction arguments and possible ways of making Ontic's induction mechanisms more powerful are discussed in section 3.2.2.

2.3   Inference Mechanisms Unlike Ontic's

This section surveys some of the general purpose inference mechanisms that have been introduced in the past thirty years and compares these mechanisms with Ontic's object-oriented inference mechanisms. Only general purpose inference mechanisms are discussed here; domain specific mechanisms, such as Chou's application of Wu's method for geometry theorem proving, will not be discussed [WU86] [CHOU84]. I will also not discuss decision procedures for particular theories or mechanisms for combining decision procedures [NELS79] [SHST82].

This section briefly discusses some particular general purpose inference systems. The Automath proof verification systems used normalization of the typed lambda calculus as an inference mechanism. The Davis-Putnam procedure was based on a direct enumeration of the Herbrand universe for a set of first order sentences. The resolution procedure and its variants improved on the Davis-Putnam procedure by introducing unification, thereby allowing a large number of ground inferences to be abbreviated with a single resolution step. The Boyer-Moore theorem prover finds induction proofs for verifying equations concerning recursive programs in pure Lisp. The Boyer-Moore theorem prover is based on user-defined (and machine verified) rewrite rules together with heuristics for generalizing induction hypotheses. The Knuth-Bendix procedure provides a way of converting a set of unordered equations into a set of rewrite rules for canonicalizing expressions. The Knuth-Bendix procedure can also be used for proving certain equations about recursive programs via an "inductionless" induction technique. Finally, a fair number of systems have been constructed which use automated theorem proving support to verify natural deduction proofs.

2.3.1   Automath

The typed lambda calculus is closely related to intuitionistic (constructive) proof theory. The analogy between typed lambda calculus and intuitionistic proof theory is based on viewing types as formulas and viewing a term of type τ as a proof of τ (where τ is viewed as a formula). If the formulas encoded by types include quantifiers, i.e., if the type system has dependent types, then it can be difficult to determine if a term u has type τ. More specifically, determining if u has type τ may involve normalizing (i.e. evaluating) the term u. This normalization process can be viewed as inference where β reductions correspond to either the inference rule of modus-ponens or the inference rule of universal instantiation.

The relationship between types and formulas of intuitionistic logic underlies one of the earlier mathematical verification systems, the Au-

tomath system [DBRJ68], [DBRJ73]. The Automath system has been
used to verify Landau's Grundlagen, a book on the foundations of the
integers, rationals, reals, and complex numbers [JTTG79]. The book includes a very rigorous (almost formal) definition of each number system.
The rationals are defined as equivalences classes of pairs of integers, the
reals are defined as Dedekind cuts in the rationals, the complex numbers
are defined as pairs of reals. The book also includes proofs that the basic
algebraic operations on these numbers are well defined (e.g. addition of
rationals, multiplication of reals). No significant theorems are proven
other than the well-formedness of these basic definitions.

Even though Landau's grundlagen is an extremely rigorous (almost
formal) book, the version of the book readable by the Automath system
is about ten times as long as the Grundlagen itself. This indicates that
the Automath verifier does not use powerful automatic inference mechanisms; there is not yet good evidence that normalization of the typed
lambda calculus is a useful automated inference mechanism.

2.3.2   The Davis-Putnam Procedure

The Davis-Putnam procedure [DAVS60] is based directly on Herbrand's
theorem for the first order predicate calculus. Herbrand's theorem implies that if Σ is an unsatisfiable set of first order formulas in Skolem
normal form then there exists a *finite* set Γ of *ground instantiations* of Σ
such that Γ is inconsistent. It is possible to write a computer program
that decides whether a set of ground formulas is consistent. To determine if the original set Σ of first order formulas is satisfiable, one can
simply enumerate all finite ground instantiations Γ of Σ and test each
one for consistency. If Σ is inconsistent then by Herbrand's theorem one
will find a ground instantiation Γ of Σ that is inconsistent.

The Davis-Putnam procedure is not used today; resolution is more
effective [ROBN65]. The Davis-Putnam procedure spends most of its
time determining the satisfiability of quantifier-free formulas. Resolution theorem proving is more effective because a large (infinite) number
of of ground inferences are summarized in a single resolution step. More
specifically, the formula generated by a resolution step can be viewed
as a universally quantified lemma which summarizes a large number of
ground statements [ROBN65]. Because other proof mechanisms (resolution) are more effective than the Davis-Putnam procedure, the Davis-
Putnam procedure will not be discussed further here.

2.3.3   Resolution and its Variants

Most research in automated theorem proving in the past twenty years
has been based in some way on resolution. The basic resolution rule was
introduced by Robinson in 1965 and shown to be refutation complete
for first order predicate calculus [ROBN65]. The resolution principle
represented a clear advance over the Davis-Putnam procedure because
a single resolution step abbreviates a large number of the ground inferences. However the number of possible n-step deductions grows expo-
nentially in n and it soon became clear that resolution theorem provers
could not, in practice, find significant theorems by searching this large
space of possible deductions.

The late sixties saw the development of a large number of restrictions on the resolution principle. Each such restriction rules out certain
resolution steps and thus reduces the number of possible n-step deductions. In spite of the reduction in the number of possible inferences,
various restricted forms of resolution are logically complete. A description of various restrictions and modifications of the resolution rule can be
found in [LVLD78]. Connection graph resolution, a resolution restriction
invented by Kowalski, is described in [BIBL81].

One perceived difficulty with resolution theorem proving, in addition
to the large search spaces encountered, is the use of normal forms. Resolution requires that first order formulas be put in normal from in three
stages. First, all quantifiers are moved to the beginning of the formula
resulting in a formula in *prenex normal form*. Second, existential quantifiers are replaced by skolem functions resulting in an equisatisfiable
formula in prenex normal form with only universal quantifiers. Finally,
the matrix of the formula (the part after the quantifiers) must be placed
in conjunctive normal form resulting in a set of universally quantified
clauses where each clause is a disjunction of literals. Several researchers
have developed theorem proving techniques which are similar to resolution but which do not require the last normalization step: the matrix
of the formula need not be in conjunctive normal form. Such "non-
clausal" provers are described in [ANDR81], [MURR82], and [STIC82].
These non-clausal procedures are similar to resolution in that they use
unification to find matches between formulas and matched formulas are
combined to generate new formulas. The non-clausal procedures are
also similar to resolution in that existential quantification is eliminated

in favor of Skolem constants.

Research in resolution theorem proving and related techniques has focused on establishing logical completeness. However, logical completeness may not be important in practice. The Boyer-Moore theorem prover is clearly not complete, it often terminates in failure, and yet the Boyer-Moore prover has been been used effectively in more applications than has any other theorem proving system.

As a side effect of focusing on completeness, the resolution theorem proving community has failed to make any distinction between "obvious" and "non-obvious" inferences. The failure to distinguish obvious and non-obvious inferences makes it difficult to use resolution theorem provers in interactive proof verifiers. Any interactive proof verifier based on resolution must have some way of forcing the resolution process to terminate so that a proposed proof step can be rejected in a finite amount of time. For example, Bledsoe built an interactive verifier which simply imposed a time limit on the resolution process [BLED72]. A more principled restriction of the resolution process has been introduced by Davis [DAVS81] and used in the Mizar system [TRYB85]. However the restriction proposed by Davis forces the decision procedure for obvious inferences to determine the satisfiability of an arbitrary set of ground clauses. Determining the satisfiability of a set of ground clauses is known to be NP-complete. Furthermore, as far as I know, there has never been a detailed comparison of natural arguments and theorems provable under Davis' suggestion.

2.3.4   Rewriting Mechanisms

Automated inference systems often have a hard time dealing with equality and equational axioms. Directed rewrite systems provide one approach to reasoning about equality. The process of rewriting expressions is also known as *simplification, symbolic evaluation* or *demodulation.* Rewrite systems iteratively simplify a given expression until it is in canonical form. A statement can be proved by rewriting it to the constant **true**.

Some of the most effective theorem proving systems are based on rewrite mechanisms. Most notably, the Boyer-Moore theorem prover uses a simplification mechanism guided by user defined (but machine verified) rewrite rules [BOYR79]. The Boyer-Moore theorem prover has been used to verify a wide variety of theorems from number theory, recursive function theory, formal logic and the verification of both hardware and software systems [BOYR84], [SHNK85], [RUSS85], [BOYR86]. The power of the Boyer-Moore prover comes from its ability to perform induction proofs. However the simplification (rewrite) mechanism is central to the system.

The Boyer-Moore prover is primarily used to prove equations between terms defined in pure Lisp. Once an equation has been proven it is treated as a rewrite rule to be used in future proofs. The direction of each newly proven rewrite rule is provided by the human user, e.g. when the system proves an equation $s = t$ the human user specifies whether this equation should be treated as $s \rightarrow t$, which rewrites s to t, or as $t \rightarrow s$, which rewrites t to s.

Ketonen's EKL system is another example, of a verification system based on user defined rewrite rules [KTNN84]. As in the Boyer-Moore prover, the direction of EKL rewrite rules are specified by the human user. Unlike the Boyer-Moore prover however, the EKL system uses Huet's higher order unification procedure to perform induction proofs. The EKL system lacks the facility for generalizing induction hypotheses used in the Boyer-Moore prover.

Knuth and Bendix developed a powerful method for constructing decision procedures for certain equational theories [KNTH69]. Unlike the Boyer-Moore prover and the EKL system, the Knuth-Bendix procedure can be used to *automatically* convert undirected equations to directed rewrite rules. More specifically, equations can be ordered via a general (but user specified) order $\succ$ on terms. If $s \succ t$ then the equation $s = t$ becomes the rule $s \rightarrow t$; if $t \succ s$ then the equation $s = t$ becomes $t \rightarrow s$. The partial order $\succ$ used in the Knuth-Bendix procedure must be well founded, respect term structure, and obey substitutions (see [KNTH69] for details).

After ordering equations into rewrite rules, the Knuth-Bendix procedure can also be used to automatically construct additional "derived" rewrite rules. More specifically, given a set of unordered equations, and an acceptable partial order $\succ$ on terms, the Knuth-Bendix procedure both converts equations to rewrite rules and constructs additional rewrite rules whose validity follows from the original equations. The set of rewrite rules that results from applying the Knuth-Bendix procedure to a set of Σ is often much larger than Σ. If the Knuth-Bendix procedure terminates with success it generates a set of rewrite rules that completely

canonicalize expressions relative to the given equations; by canonicalizing expressions one can determine if two terms can be proven equal from
the original set of equations. Unfortunately, however, the Knuth-Bendix
procedure does not always succeed; it can either terminate in failure or
fail to terminate.

The Knuth-Bendix procedure has been used extensively in system that
manipulate equational specifications of computer programs [KAPR86]
[LSCN86] [HUET86]. These systems are based on an equational view
of programming in which computer data structures are viewed as terms
constructed from atomic symbols (Lisp atoms) and "data constructor
functions" such as the Lisp function CONS. Recursive functions can be
defined via equations involving the defined function symbols [GTTG78]
[ODON85].

The Knuth-Bendix procedure can also be used to generate "induction
arguments" of the type performed by the Boyer-Moore theorem prover
[HUET83]. More specifically, consider the closed (variable free) terms
which can be constructed from a set of "atoms" (constructor functions
of no arguments), constructor functions (functions such as CONS which
construct data objects), and defined functions. A "data object" is a
term with no defined functions. Let Σ be a set of equations which *defines*
the defined function symbols as operations on the data objects, i.e. no
two data objects can be proven equal from Σ and every closed term
involving defined functions can be proven (under Σ) to be equal to some
data object. Now suppose we wish to prove some equation $s = t$ where
s and t are distinct terms involving defined functions and free variables.
For example, the equation $s = t$ might state the associativity of the
APPEND function on lists. The equation $s = t$ holds in the data object
universe just in case there is no counter example, i.e. no ground variable
substitution σ such that $\sigma(s)$ denotes a different data object from $\sigma(t)$.
If there exists a counterexample to the equation $s = t$ then adding this
equation to Σ would allow one to prove an equation between two distinct
data objects. The Knuth-Bendix procedure can be used (in some cases)
to convert $\Sigma \cup \{s = t\}$ to a complete set of rewrite rules. By examining
this set of rewrite rules it is possible to determine whether $\Sigma \cup \{s = t\}$
allows one to prove an equation between distinct data objects. If such an
equation is provable then the equation $s = t$ has a counterexample. If no
such equation between distinct data objects is provable from $\Sigma \cup \{s = t\}$
then the equation $s = t$ has no counterexamples and must be true in

```
(IN-CONTEXT ((LET-BE L (AND-TYPE DISTRIBUTIVE-LATTICE
                                 BOUNDED-LATTICE))
            (LET-BE X (IN-U-SET L))
            (PUSH-GOAL
              (AT-MOST-ONE (COMPLEMENT-OF X L))))

    (IN-CONTEXT ((SUPPOSE (EXISTS (COMPLEMENT-OF X L)))
                (LET-BE Y1 (COMPLEMENT-OF X L))
                (LET-BE Y2 (COMPLEMENT-OF X L)))
      (NOTE-GOAL))

    (NOTE-GOAL))
```

$$y_1 = y_1 \wedge 1 \qquad\qquad \text{A previously established fact.}$$

$$= y_1 \wedge (y_2 \vee x) \qquad\qquad \text{Because } y_2 \text{ is a complement of } x.$$

$$= (y_1 \wedge y_2) \vee (y_1 \wedge x) \qquad\qquad \text{By definition of a distributive lattice.}$$

$$= (y_1 \wedge y_2) \vee 0 \qquad\qquad \text{Because } y_1 \text{ is a complement of } x.$$

$$= (y_1 \wedge y_2) \vee (y_2 \wedge x) \qquad\qquad \text{Because } y_2 \text{ is a complement of } x.$$

$$= (y_2 \wedge y_1) \vee (y_2 \wedge x) \qquad\qquad \text{Because } \wedge \text{ is commutative.}$$

$$= y_2 \wedge (y_1 \vee x) \qquad\qquad \text{By definition of a distributive lattice.}$$

$$= y_2 \wedge 1 \qquad\qquad \text{Because } y_1 \text{ is a complement of } x.$$

$$= y_2 \qquad\qquad \text{Because } y_2 = y_2 \wedge 1$$

Figure 2.2
A statement that is obvious to Ontic but not obvious to people together with the
equational reasoning chain found by Ontic's congruence closure mechanism

the data object universe. In general it may be possible to show that
$s = t$ has counterexamples at an intermediate point in the Knuth-Bendix
procedure; thus a complete set of rewrite rules for $\Sigma \cup \{s = t\}$ may not
be required.

One problem with the Knuth-Bendix procedure however is the need for
a single partial order on all expressions. There may be domain specific
intuitions about how terms should be rewritten and it is difficult to
incorporate such knowledge into a single uniform term ordering. While

some sophisticated partial orders have been developed [DRSH79], it is not yet clear whether a uniform term ordering can be used for the large verifications that have been done with the Boyer-Moore prover.

Like unification research, research on term rewriting systems using the Knuth-Bendix mechanism has centered on the notion of logical completeness. There are many equational theories with an undecidable set of equational consequences and in such cases the Knuth-Bendix procedure either terminates in failure or fails to terminate. When using the Knuth-Bendix procedure it is not clear what to do when the procedure fails. Even if a complete set of reductions is found, the time required to perform the rewriting may be prohibitively large. The rigid framework of the Knuth-Bendix procedure may make it difficult to perform the large verifications that have been done with the Boyer-Moore prover; it is not clear that a Knuth-Bendix based system could verify the RSA encryption algorithm or the undecidability of the halting problem as has been done with the Boyer-Moore prover [BOYR84] [BOYR86].

Rewrite systems are designed to handle equational theories. The Ontic system handles equality with its congruence closure mechanism; rewrite rules are not used. The congruence closure mechanism can be quite powerful in practice. Figure 2.1 gives an example of an inference done using Ontic's congruence closure mechanism. Consider a distributive lattice with a least member 0 and a greatest member 1 (a lattice with a least and greatest member is called *bounded*). If x and y are members of the lattice L then we say that x and y are complements if the meet of x and y is 0 and the join of x and y is 1. It was obvious to the Ontic interpreter that in any bounded distributive lattice a given member x has at most one complement. Ontic's proof of this fact, also shown in figure 2.1, uses congruence closure.

Figure 2.1 shows that congruence closure is a powerful technique for reasoning about equality. Because Ontic handles equality with congruence closure rather than rewrite rules, there is no need for the user to specify rewrite directions for equations; the Ontic system can handle undirected declarative equations. The value of declarative as opposed to procedural representations is discussed in more detail in section 2.4.2.

2.3.5   Natural Deduction Systems

Natural deduction systems are based on "natural" rules of inference. A given rule says that a goal G of a certain form can be proven by reducing the goal G to the subgoals $G_1, G_2 \ldots G_n$. Different rules provide different ways of achieving a goal where the success of any one rule is sufficient. The earliest natural deduction system was Newell, Shaw and Simon's Logic Theorist [NEWL57]. This system used natural deduction rules and backward chaining to prove theorems in Whitehead and Russell's Principia Mathematica. Soon after the construction of the Logic Theorist, Gelernter constructed his program for finding proofs in Euclidean geometry [GLRT59]. Gelernter's system also used backward chaining and natural deduction rules but the subgoals were pruned by the use of a diagram, i.e. a model of the assumptions in the proof. If a subgoal was false in the diagram then the system could infer that the subgoal could not be achieved and thus should be abandoned.

During the sixties research in automatic theorem proving focused primarily on resolution theorem proving. However, during the early seventies frustration with resolution systems lead to a renewed interest in natural deduction systems [BLED77]. Natural deduction systems from the seventies include [BLED72], [NEVN74], [RETR73], [ERNS73], [GLDS73], [BLED73], and [DKLR77]. These later natural deduction systems often used resolution as a subroutine for proving subgoals. A time limit was imposed on resolution proofs to force the resolution theorem prover to terminate quickly [BLED72].

One of the major problems with using resolution as a test for "obvious" subgoals was the tendency of resolution to get lost when it was given too many initial facts. In other words resolution was not able to automatically find the relevant facts in a large lemma library. As Bledsoe says in [BLED72]:

> One of the more serious [problems is referencing]. The computer should be able to bring to bear "all it knows" (all definition axioms and previously proven theorems) ... But if one attempts a resolution proof on a large number of formulas, the result is the production of a glut of irrelevant clauses and sure failure, even when the best known search strategies are used. Thus the crucial part of a resolution proof is the *selection* of the reference theorems by the *human* user; the human, by this one action, usually employs more skill than that used by the computer in the proof.

It is useful to remember that this was written in 1971, well after most of the refinements to resolution had been developed. These comments about the ineffectiveness of resolution on large lemma libraries are probably as true today as they were in 1971. The Ontic interpreter on the other hand seems to handle large lemma libraries without difficulty. It would be interesting to reconstruct these old natural deduction systems using the Ontic interpreter rather than resolution to test for obvious subgoals.

The seventies also saw a development of basic natural deduction proof checking systems that did not provide much automated reasoning support. For example, McDonald and Suppes developed an interactive proof checking system for teaching an introductory logic course [MCDN84]. Richard Weyhrauch also developed the FOL system for checking first order logic proofs [WEYH77].

While the FOL system does not provide sophisticated general purpose theorem proving, it does provide a uniform mechanism for associating any given predicate or function symbol with a computer program for computing the value of the predicate or function on "semantic" arguments. It seems clear that mathematical verification systems could benefit from the addition of computational oracles. Along with procedures for basic arithmetic (addition, multiplication etc.) one can imagine incorporating procedures for symbolic integration, series summation, or polynomial manipulation. No attempt has been made to incorporate such features into the Ontic system.

Procedural attachment is part of a general focus on "metatheory" within the FOL system [WEYH80]. While procedural attachment has clear potential value, I think the emphasis on metatheory is misplaced. There seems to be a fundamental unity in all mathematics; there is no fundamental distinction between "metamathematics", number theory, graph theory, finite combinatorics, or real analysis. A system which reason about numbers, graphs, and ordered sets can just as easily reason about formulas, models, and Tarskian truth functions.

During the late seventies, and into the eighties, there has been an emphasis on "programmable" natural deduction systems. These systems provide a mechanism for adding user defined inference rules. The first such programmable system was Edinburgh LCF [GRDN79]. A more recent programmable natural deduction system is the Nuprl system developed by Bates and Constable [CNST86] [HOWE86]. The Nuprl system grew out of research in interactive verifications systems [CNST82] and their use in teaching formal logic and formal approaches to program verification. The Nuprl system is based on constructive type theory and places particular emphasis on finding constructive proofs. The system provides a facility for converting a constructive proof that a certain number exists into a program for computing that number.

Backward chaining natural deduction systems use rules of inference to convert a given goal to a set of subgoals. In the Nuprl system the user can define new inference rules, or "tactics", for converting a goal to a set of subgoals. When a tactic replaces a goal G by a set of subgoals G_1, G_2, ... G_n the tactic must construct a proof showing that the replacement is sound, i.e. that the subgoals G_1, G_2, ... G_n imply the goal G. One could write a tactic for showing that any given set S is a subset of U by supposing that S is non-empty and then considering an arbitrary member of S. One could then use this tactic as a subroutine and write another tactic for showing that two sets are equal by showing that each is a subset of the other. In the Ontic system one has to repeat this style of argument every time one wants to prove set equality. It seems likely that tactics could be used in the Ontic system to reduce the length of machine readable proofs. On the other hand it seems likely that Ontic's object oriented inference mechanisms could be used to reduce the length of proofs in the Nuprl system.

2.4 Issues in Automated Reasoning

There are several general issues involved in the construction of proof verification systems. First, in designing a verification system one should consider the expressive power of the formal language involved. Does the language allow one to express a wide variety of formal concepts and arguments? Second, one should consider the extent to which the knowledge base contains procedural as opposed to declarative information. Procedural information may help make the system run more effectively but procedural information is harder to construct and a reliance on procedural information makes automatic discovery of useful information more difficult. Third, one should consider whether the system should rely on backward or forward chaining. It is not clear whether forward chaining has any intrinsic advantage over backward chaining or vice versa. In both cases the basic problem is to control the generation of facts or subgoals. Simplification seems to be effective as a guiding principle in backward chaining while focus seems to be effective as a guiding principle in forward chaining.

2.4.1 Expressive Power

Some very restricted formal languages have tractable inference problems: there exists a tractable procedure for determining the validity of any statement expressible in the language. Thus there seems to be a tradeoff between expressive power and computational tractability in knowledge representation languages [LVSQ85]. However this "trade off" is misleading. In order to design a language with a tractable inference problem one must design a language in which hard questions cannot be asked. But this does not produce the result one really wants; rather than making it easier to answer hard questions, limiting the expressive power of a language simply makes it impossible to *ask* hard questions. On the other hand, increasing the expressive power of the reasoning language can make it easier to reason about hard questions.

Natural mathematics (mathematics done in English) seems to have a notion of a "well typed" expression. For example, consider the well typed phrase "the value of the map f on the point x" as opposed to the garbled phrase "the value of topological space X on the point x". The notion of a well typed natural phrase seems to correspond to the notion of a well typed formal expression. Mathematicians talk about groups, rings, fields, topological spaces, differentiable manifolds, group homomorphisms, differentiable maps and much more. It seems that in natural mathematics any definable set (or class) can be used as a type in determining the set of well typed phrases. Most strongly typed formal systems, however, do not allow arbitrary predicates to be used as types.

In designing a type system there appears to be a trade off between expressive power and computational tractability. One can ensure computational tractability by restricting the type system so that only certain simple predicates can be used as types. Restricted type systems cannot express natural types such as "prime number", "symmetric matrix", or "transitive reduced graph". While the inability to express such types makes type-checking tractable, it prevents the type-checking process from even attempting to verify certain semantic properties of programs. It seems likely that one could construct a quickly terminating type-checking procedure which could verify all simple types and could also verify *some* more difficult "semantic" types. Restrictions on the vocabulary of types does not make it easier to answer hard questions, it only makes hard questions impossible to ask.

2.4.2 Declarative Representations

Many automated inference systems require every declarative fact to be augmented with procedural information: information about how the declarative fact is to be used in the inference process. Purely declarative facts, facts not augmented with procedural instructions, have the advantage that they are easier to generate — it seems easier for people to write down a set of purely declarative facts than to write down both the declarative facts and additional information about how those facts are to be used. The ease of generating purely declarative facts may be particularly important in discovery systems — systems which automatically generate new lemmas. The task of discovering and using new facts is easier if one does not have to specify procedural information each time a new fact is discovered.

Unfortunately, purely declarative facts have the disadvantage that they are more difficult to compute with. Ketonen has discussed the difficulty of constructing effective theorem provers that use purely declarative information [KTNN84]. In supporting the use of procedural information Ketonen considers the following formula:

$$P(x) \Rightarrow A = B$$

He argues that there is no single way to use this formula and lists the following possible procedural interpretations:

1. Replace $P(x) \Rightarrow A = B$ by **true** whenever it appears.

2. Replace $A = B$ by **true** if one can prove $P(x)$ in the current situation.

3. Replace $P(x)$ by *false* if one can prove $A \neq B$.

4. Replace A by B whenever one can prove $P(x)$.

5. Replace B by A whenever one can prove $P(x)$.

6. Replace A by B whenever one can prove $P(x)$ but not in terms resulting from this substitution.

Ketonen argues that one must choose between the above procedural interpretations. Interpretations (4) and (5) seem opposite in intent. Furthermore formulas involving quantifiers would have an even greater number of different interpretations. Ketonen concludes that the user must specify how formulas are to be used.

It seems that Ketonen's difficulty with purely declarative representation comes from his commitment to rewrite systems. Ontic's inference mechanism effectively uses interpretations (1) through (5) simultaneously. Replacing a formula Φ by **true** in a rewrite system is analogous to putting the label **true** on the node for Φ in the Ontic's marker propagation mechanism. In the Ontic system Boolean constraint propagation handles the procedural interpretations (1) through (3) above. In the Ontic system equalities between nodes are represented by giving those nodes the same color label. This representation of equality together with the congruence closure mechanism effectively handles both procedural interpretations (4) and (5). The 6th procedural interpretation seems a little strange and is not handled in the Ontic system — congruence closure effectively performs all substitutions.

One of the primary features of the Knuth-Bendix procedure is that equations are automatically converted to rewrite rules using a single partial order that is defined for all terms. Thus, once the partial order has been defined, purely declarative equations are automatically given procedural interpretations. However the Knuth-Bendix procedure is not guaranteed to succeed: it may terminate without producing a complete set of rewrite rules or it may run forever in attempting to generate such a set. Furthermore, because the Knuth-Bendix procedure produces rewrite rules, it must choose either procedural interpretation (4) or interpretation (5) — the Ontic system effectively does both simultaneously. The effectiveness of the Knuth-Bendix procedure in large verification applications has not yet been established.

Further experimentation is needed to see if systems which use purely declarative information, such as Ontic, can be made as effective as systems which are based on rewrite rules, such as the Boyer-Moore theorem prover.

2.4.3   Forward Chaining

Forward chaining systems start with a set of premises and derive conclusions from those premises. Backward chaining systems start with a goal and reduce that goal to subgoals. It is not clear whether forward chaining has any intrinsic advantage over backward chaining or vice versa. In both cases the basic problem is to control the generation of facts or subgoals. Both forward chaining and backward chaining systems can become swamped in a sea of derived facts or derived subgoals. Certain sources of guidance seem to work for backward chaining and other sources of guidance seem to work for forward chaining.

Simplicity seems to work as a guiding principle in backward chaining. Rewrite systems are backward chaining because they start with the expression to be proved and rewrite that expression in an attempt to show it equivalent to the constant **true**. Rewrite systems are guided by some notion of simplicity: a goal expression is always replaced by a simpler goal. The notion of simplicity is either implicit in the user specified rewrite rules, as in the Boyer-Moore prover, or explicitly defined as an ordering on expressions, as in Knuth-Bendix based systems. In both cases however a notion of simplicity guides the generation of subgoals.

Focus seems to work as a guiding principle in forward chaining. Ontic's object oriented inference mechanisms are guided by the restriction that derived facts must be about the focus objects. A similar restriction is used in other forward chaining systems such as Nevins' geometry theorem prover [NEVN74], constraint systems such as Waltz labeling [WLTZ75], and constraint languages such as that described by Sussman and Steele [SUSS80].

It should be possible to integrate both backward and forward chaining in a single system. In such a system simplification should be used as a guiding principle in backward chaining and focus should be used as a guiding principle in forward chaining.

3 Ontic as a Cognitive Model

One can attempt to evaluate Ontic as a model of human mathematical cognition by comparing the formal "proofs" that are acceptable to the Ontic system with the natural language proofs that are acceptable to people. There are some clear differences between Ontic proofs and natural arguments. In certain cases the Ontic system can verify proof steps that are not obvious to people; we say that Ontic exhibits superhuman performance. In other cases there are statements which are obvious to people but which require multistep proofs in the Ontic system; we say that Ontic exhibits subhuman performance. The superhuman performance and much of the subhuman performance indicate ways in which the Ontic system might be modified to yield a better cognitive model.

Ontic's congruence closure mechanism provides a clear example of superhuman performance. The Ontic system can use its congruence closure mechanism to "see" that in a distributive lattice complements are unique. This fact is not obvious to people. The Ontic proof of the Stone representation theorem relies on proofs of a series lattice theoretic identities which were obvious to the Ontic system but not to human mathematicians. These identities included de Morgan's laws which were proven from the algebraic axioms for a Boolean lattice.

It is possible to modify the Ontic system in a way that eliminates superhuman behavior while preserving most of the inferential power of the system. Unlike the current Ontic system, the modified version has a straightforward implementation on a very fast parallel architecture. The elimination of superhuman behavior and the provision for a highly parallel implementation yield a more plausible cognitive model.

Of course, Ontic also exhibits subhuman performance. Some cases of subhuman performance in the proof of the Stone representation theorem can be traced to weaknesses in the lemma library. A more significant set of examples of subhuman performance involves mathematical induction. Although the Ontic system can be used to verify induction arguments, the expansion factor is large. In natural mathematics induction arguments are often unstated and unnoticed even though people understand the arguments and agree to their validity. For example consider a graph where the nodes of the graph are colored such that any two nodes with an arc between them have the same color. Clearly if nodes n and m have different colors then there is no path between them in the graph. To verify this fact with the Ontic system would require an induction on the length of paths. There are many other examples from both mathe-

matics and common sense where induction arguments seem to be done
at a subconscious level.

Future experimentation will certainly turn up additional ways in which
the Ontic system exhibits subhuman performance. Hopefully examples
of subhuman performance will lead to the discovery of additional inference mechanisms that bring the system closer to human ability in
verifying natural arguments.

3.1   Superhuman Performance

Congruence closure accounts for all the examples of superhuman performance of the Ontic system. The Ontic proof of the Stone representation
theorem contains six examples of superhuman performance based on
congruence closure [MCAL87]. All of these examples involve reasoning
about lattice identities.

The first example of superhuman Ontic performance is the proof, discussed in chapter 2, that in a distributive lattice complements are unique.
The second example is the proof of de Morgan's laws for complemented
distributive lattices. De Morgan's laws are straightforward if one assumes that Boolean operations have their standard meaning as operators on sets, or equivalently, if Boolean operations have their standard
meaning as operations on truth functions. However, until one has proven
the Stone representation theorem, one must consider the possibility that
there exist pathological complemented distributive lattices in which the
Boolean operations cannot be viewed as operations on sets or as truth
functions. The super-human Ontic proof of de Morgan's laws and an
analysis of that proof are shown in figure 3.1.

The Ontic proof of the Stone representation theorem relies on a proof
that for any elements x and y of a complemented distributive lattice the
following are equivalent:

1. $x \leq y$

2. $y^* \leq x^*$

3. $x \wedge y^* = 0$

4. $x^* \vee y = 1$

```
(IN-CONTEXT ((LET-BE B BOOLEAN-LATTICE)
             (LET-BE X (IN-U-SET B))
             (LET-BE Y (IN-U-SET B))
             (LET-BE CX (COMPLEMENT X B))
             (LET-BE CY (COMPLEMENT Y B))
             (LET-BE M (MEET X Y B))
             (LET-BE J (JOIN CX CY B)))
      (NOTE (IS J (COMPLEMENT-OF M B)))))
```

Let x^* and y^* be the complements of x and y respectively. Let m be the meet of x and y and let j be the join of x^* and y^*. We must show that m and j are compliments, i.e. that $m \wedge j = 0$ and $m \vee j = 1$. This can be done as follows:

$$m \wedge (x^* \vee y^*) = (m \wedge x^*) \vee (m \wedge y^*) \qquad \text{By distributivity of } \wedge \text{ over } \vee.$$
$$= ((x \wedge x^*) \wedge y) \vee ((y \wedge y^*) \wedge x) \qquad \text{By assoc. and comm. of } \wedge.$$
$$= (0 \wedge y) \vee (0 \wedge x) \qquad \text{By definition of complement.}$$
$$= 0 \qquad \text{By algebraic properties of 0.}$$

$$(x \wedge y) \vee j \quad = (x \vee j) \wedge (y \vee j) \qquad \text{By distributivity of } \vee \text{ over } \wedge.$$
$$= (y^* \vee (x^* \vee x)) \wedge (x^* \vee (y^* \vee y)) \qquad \text{By assoc. and comm. of } \vee.$$
$$= (y^* \vee 1) \vee (x^* \vee 1) \qquad \text{By definition of complement.}$$
$$= 1 \qquad \text{By algebraic properties of 1.}$$

Figure 3.1
An example of a superhuman Ontic proof and a corresponding natural argument.

The Ontic proof of the equivalence of these four facts is done by showing that 1) $\Rightarrow$ 2) $\Rightarrow$ 3) $\Rightarrow$ 4) $\Rightarrow$ 1). This is done in a context where the uniqueness of complements and de Morgan's laws have already been established. For each implication there is a set of four focus objects which makes the implication obvious to the Ontic system. The proof of each implication shows superhuman performance involving congruence closure.

3.1.1 A Very Fast Parallel Architecture

This section proposes an architecture for massively parallel computation and argues that, unlike Boolean constraint propagation, congruence clo-

sure is difficult to implement on this architecture[1]. People make truth
judgments about obvious statements in about a second. Although the
computation performed by neurons is not well understood, it is clear
that neurons run very slowly. It seems likely that neurons would require
one to ten milliseconds to compute the logical and of two Boolean signals. If people are computing truth judgments with Boolean circuitry,
and if the gate delay for neuronal hardware is on the order of one to ten
milliseconds, then people make truth judgments about obvious statements in 100 to 1000 gate delays. Computing complex truth judgments
in only 100 to 1000 gate delays requires massive parallelism.

Consider a finite state machine where the state of the machine at time
i is given by an n-bit bit vector D_i. The state transition table of the
machine can be given by a Boolean circuit Φ of n inputs and n outputs
where the state transitions of the machine are governed by the equation

$$D_{i+1} \;=\; \Phi(D_i)$$

To make the finite state machine run quickly the Boolean circuit Φ
should have low depth, say ten gates. If Φ has depth ten then a state
transition can be computed in ten gate delays. However, the bit vector
defining the state of the machine can be very large: millions or tens of
millions of bits, and the circuit Φ can involve millions or tens of millions
of gates.

It seems possible to compile an Ontic graph into a Boolean circuit
governing a finite state machine. More specifically, a labeling of an
Ontic graph could be encoded in the state bit vector of the machine. The
basic inference operations on graph labels could be incorporated into a
Boolean circuit Φ governing state transitions. Two bits are needed for
each formula node to represent the three possible labeling states of the
node: true, false and unknown. Boolean constraints on formula nodes
could be compiled directly in the structure of the Boolean circuit Φ.
Every node in an Ontic graph is also associated with a color label. The
color label for a given node in the graph could be represented with a
set of bits in the machine's state vector. The Boolean circuit governing

---

[1]It is easy to show that Boolean constraint propagation is polynomial time complete and thus "unparallelizable"; the worst case running time on a parallel machine
is linear in the size of the graph. In many cases however, a parallel implementation
would run much faster than a serial implementation; a parallel implementation runs
in time proportional to the longest single inference chain while a serial implementation runs in time proportional to the total number of inferences.

state transitions could be designed in such a way that if an equation node became true then the color labels of the equated nodes at time $i+1$ would each be set to the maximum of the two labels at time i. In this way the color labels could be made to respect the truth of equality formulas. With the exception of congruence closure, all of the inference techniques used in the Ontic system seem to be amenable to a massively parallel implementation in a low-depth Boolean circuit governing a finite state machine.

Ontic's implementation of congruence closure uses a hash table to map color tuples to colors. In order to implement a hash table one needs to be able to compute memory addresses for a random access memory. The use of a hash table seems incompatible with an implementation based on a low depth Boolean circuit governing a large finite state machine.

Congruence closure can be replaced with substitution constraints as described in the next section. Substitution constraints are Boolean constraints involving equality formulas; such constraints can be compiled directly into a low-depth Boolean circuit governing a finite state machine.

3.1.2 Substitution Constraints

Substitution constraints provide an alternative to congruence closure for reasoning about equality. Substitution constraints rely on Boolean constraint propagation's ability to handle certain equality inferences. Boolean constraint propagation ensures a simple relationship between the truth of equality formulas and the color labels encoding equivalence. Boolean constraint propagation, however, does not automatically handle the substitution of equals for equals; in the Ontic system substitution is handled by congruence closure. On the other hand, Boolean constraint propagation can be made to handle substitution by adding certain Boolean constraints which I will call substitution constraints. Boolean constraint propagation with substitution constraints is weaker than congruence closure in that it generates fewer obvious truths in a given context.

As a simple example of a substitution constraint consider a term $f(c)$ which consists of an operator f applied to a specific argument c. We can assume that the operator f is defined on objects of a certain type τ and that c is an instance of τ. Suppose that g is a generic individual of type τ. To ensure that inheritance works properly one can add the

Boolean constraint

$$g = c \;\Rightarrow\; f(g) = f(c)$$

Now if the system ever generates a binding $g \mapsto c$ then g and c will get the same color label and Boolean constraint propagation will ensure that the equation $g = c$ gets labeled true and thus, by the above substitution constraint, the equation $f(g) = f(c)$ will be labeled true. Independent of congruence closure, if $f(g)$ has the same color label as $f(c)$ then certain facts about $f(g)$ can be inherited by $f(c)$. For example if $f(g)$ is known to be an instance of a type σ then $f(c)$ will also be known to be an instance of the type σ. Thus the above Boolean constraint allows the binding $g \mapsto c$ to cause c to inherit facts that are stated in terms of g.

Substitution constraints can be used to perform inferences based on the substitution of equals for equals. Suppose that c is known to be equal to b and consider the terms $f(c)$ and $f(b)$. Furthermore assume the graph structure underlying Boolean constraint propagation includes the following substitution constraints

$$g = c \;\Rightarrow\; f(g) = f(c)$$

$$g = b \;\Rightarrow\; f(g) = f(b)$$

Now suppose that the system focuses on c and generates the binding $g \mapsto c$. Since c and b are known to be equal, the nodes for g, c, and b will all get the same color label. Thus the equations $g = c$ and $g = b$ will become true. Thus both the equations $f(g) = f(c)$ and $f(g) = f(b)$ will become true and the nodes for $f(g)$, $f(c)$ and $f(b)$ will all get the same color label. Thus focusing on c causes the system to deduce that $f(c)$ equals $f(b)$. This scheme for handling substitution of equals for equals via substitution constraints can be suitably generalized to handle operators of more than one argument.

3.1.3   Superhuman Performance Re-Examined

The scheme for equality inference based substitution constraints is not as powerful as the full congruence closure mechanism. More specifically, using substitution constraints the substitution of equals for equals can only be done when the substituted expressions are equal to some focus object. All of the examples of superhuman performance discussed above involve substitution for non-focus objects. Figure 2.2 in chapter 2 shows the Ontic proof that complements are unique together with an expanded derivation showing how the Ontic system proved that if y_1 and y_2 are both complements of x then y_1 must equal y_2. The second line in the expanded derivation is derived by replacing 1 with $(y_2 \vee x)$ even though neither 1 nor $(y_2 \vee x)$ is a focus object. If congruence inference required focusing on the substituted expression then the second line could only be derived by focusing on $y_2 \vee x$. Similarly, line four is derived by substituting 0 for $y_1 \wedge x$ even though $y_1 \wedge x$ is not a focus object. Lines five and seven also involve substitution for non-focused expressions.

Even the weaker scheme based on substitution constraints could prove that complements are unique in a single inference step if the system focused on x, y_1, y_2, $y_2 \vee x$, $y_1 \wedge x$, $y_2 \wedge x$ and $y_2 \vee x$ all at the same time. However, it seems that people have a hard time focusing on seven objects simultaneously. The ability of the Ontic system to focus on a large number of objects simultaneously is perhaps another source of superhuman performance.

3.2 Subhuman Performance

Some parts of the Ontic proof of the Stone representation theorem exhibit subhuman performance which can be attributed, at least in part, to weaknesses in the lemma library. Other examples indicate weaknesses in the fundamental inference architecture. It is hoped that examples of subhuman performance will lead to new inference techniques which increase the usefulness of verification systems.

3.2.1 Weaknesses in the Lemma Library

The lemma library developed for Ontic's proof of the Stone representation theorem does not include a duality principle for Lattices. Given an appropriate duality principle the proof of any identity in lattice theory would lead immediately to a proof of the dual identity. For example consider de Morgan's laws. A first de Morgan law can be phrased as follows.

$$(x \vee y)^* = x^* \wedge y^*$$

A second de Morgan's law can be derived from the first via a duality principle for Boolean lattices: the result of switching $\vee$ and $\wedge$ (and 1 and 0) in any Boolean lattice identity leads to another Boolean lattice identity. Given the duality principle for Boolean lattices the validity of

the above de Morgan law leads immediately to the validity of the dual
law:

$$(x \wedge y)^* = x^* \vee y^*$$

One could incorporate the duality principle into the Ontic system by
defining the dual of a lattice. Given any lattice (or any partial order)
the dual of the lattice is defined to be that lattice which has the same
elements but in which the partial order has been reversed. Using the
Ontic system one could easily define a function which mapped any lattice
to its dual lattice. Furthermore one could prove that if L' is the dual
of a Boolean lattice L then L' is a Boolean lattice such that the meet
operation in L' equals the join operation in L, the join operation in
L' equals the meet operation of L, and L' has the same complement
operation as L. Given a Boolean lattice identity I one could then prove
that the dual identity I' must hold in an arbitrary Boolean lattice L by
considering the dual lattice L' and noting that I' holds in L just in case
the lattice identity I holds in the dual L'.

Another example where standard notions could be added to the lemma
library to reduce the length of proofs involves the algebraic character-
ization of a lattice. It turns out that the partial order of a lattice is
determined by the meet and join operations and in fact one can define
a Boolean lattice to be a set together with meet, join and complement
operations that satisfy certain equational axioms. This algebraic view of
a lattice is described in textbooks on lattice theory and could be added
to Ontic's lemma library. The algebraic view of a lattice would allow a
shorter machine readable proof of one of the lemmas used for the Stone
representation theorem. More specifically, the algebraic view of a lattice
provides a short proof that if S is a subset of a Boolean lattice L such
that S is closed under the meet, join and complement operations of L
then the set S together with the partial order of L restricted to S forms
a lattice with the same lattice operations as L.

3.2.2 Mathematical Induction

The clearest examples of subhuman behavior on the part of the Ontic
system involve mathematical induction. Many common sense inferences
appear to involve induction. Consider the following examples:

- Consider a colored graph in which adjacent nodes have the same
  color, i.e. if there is an arc between nodes n and m then n and

m have the same color. If nodes n and m have different colors then there is no path between them in the graph. A formal proof requires induction on the length of paths in the graph.

- Consider a chess board. The white pawns start on the second rank and never move backward. Therefore no white pawn can ever appear on the first rank. A formal proof of this statement requires induction on the number of steps in the game.

- Consider two containers for holding marbles. Initially each container is empty. Marbles are then placed in the containers in pairs; one marble from each pair is placed in each container. No matter how many times this is done, assuming the containers do not overflow, there will be the same number of marbles in each container. A formal proof of this statement requires an induction on the number of marbles placed in the containers.

- Consider Rubic's cube. Suppose the cube starts in a solved position and is scrambled by some number of rotations of faces of the cube. There exists a set of steps that unscrambles the cube. A formal proof of this statement requires an induction on the number of rotations used to scramble the cube.

- Consider a mouse running in a maze. Suppose the maze is arranged inside a box such that there are no openings in the walls of the box and the mouse cannot jump over the walls. No matter how long the mouse runs, and no matter where it goes inside the maze, the mouse will not get outside the box. A formal proof of this statement requires induction on the number of "moves" the mouse makes in the box.

In each of the above examples the conclusion is obvious to people. In each example, if the concepts involved were approximated by mathematically precise notions then any mathematician would accept the conclusion as obvious and would not ask for further proof.

Ontic can be used to perform induction proofs. However induction proofs must be done explicitly: one must explicitly formulate the induction hypothesis and explicitly verify the induction step. For example, consider verifying that white pawns in a game of chess cannot get to

the first rank. This fact can be verified using the following induction
principle for natural numbers.

```
(DEFTYPE SET-OF-NATNUMS
   (LAMBDA ((S SET))
      (IS-EVERY (MEMBER-OF S) NATURAL-NUMBER)))

(LEMMA
   (FORALL ((S SET-OF-NATNUMS))

      (=> (AND (IS ZERO (MEMBER-OF S))
               (FORALL ((N (MEMBER-OF S)))
                  (IS (SUCCESSOR N) (MEMBER-OF S))))

          (IS-EVERY NATURAL-NUMBER (MEMBER-OF S)))))
```

The above induction principle says that if a set S contains zero and is
closed under successor then it contains all numbers. The set S represents
an induction hypothesis; S is the set of numbers which satisfy the hypothesis. In the chess example one must prove that white pawns never end up
on the first rank. More formally, let an instance of the type CHESS-GAME
be a particular game of chess, i.e. a particular sequence of moves. If G
is a chess game and N is a number then (WHITE-PAWN-ON-BOARD G N)
denotes the type whose instances are the white pawns which are on the
chess board after the N'th move of the game G. We let (RANK-OF P G N)
be the rank occupied by the pawn P immediately after the N'th move of
the game G. Figure 3.2 contains statements which follow from the rules
of chess. An Ontic proof that pawns never get to the first rank is given
in figure 3.3. The goals in the proof are numbered and the NOTE-GOAL
steps are labeled with the number of the goal being noted. The proof
uses the facts listed in table 3.2 together with simple facts about the
ordering of natural numbers.

The proof starts by considering an arbitrary chess game G. The proof
shows that the following induction hypothesis holds for any number N.

```
(FORALL ((P (WHITE-PAWN-ON-BOARD G N)))
   (IS (RANK-OF P G N)
       (GREATER-OR-EQUAL-TO TWO)))
```

```
(FORALL ((G CHESS-GAME)
         (N NATURAL-NUMBER))
   (IS-EVERY (WHITE-PAWN-ON-BOARD G (SUCCESSOR N))
             (WHITE-PAWN-ON-BOARD G N)))

(FORALL ((G CHESS-GAME)
         (N NATURAL-NUMBER)
         (P (WHITE-PAWN-ON-BOARD G (SUCCESSOR N))))
    (IS (RANK-OF P G (SUCCESSOR N))
        (GREATER-OR-EQUAL-TO (RANK-OF P G N))))

(FORALL ((P (WHITE-PAWN-ON-BOARD G ZERO)))
   (IS (RANK-OF P G ZERO)
       (EQUAL-TO TWO)))
```

Figure 3.2
Statements which follow from the rules of chess.

The induction principle for natural numbers states that if a set of numbers contains zero and is closed under successor then it contains all numbers. If the induction hypothesis is $\Phi(N)$ then one should consider the set of all N such that $\Phi(N)$. For the above induction hypothesis one should consider the following set:

```
(THE-SET-OF-ALL
   (LAMBDA ((N NATURAL-NUMBER))
     (FORALL ((P (WHITE-PAWN-ON-BOARD G N)))
       (IS (RANK-OF P G N)
           (GREATER-OR-EQUAL-TO TWO)))))
```

The Ontic proof in figure 3.3 focuses on the set representing the induction hypothesis. It then proceeds to prove the base case and induction step. The base case uses the fact that the rank of a white pawn at time zero equals two and every number is greater than or equal to itself. In order to apply the fact that every number is greater than equal to itself one must focus on the number two. The induction step uses the fact that the rank of the pawn at time n is greater or equal to two and the rank of the pawn at time $n + 1$ is greater or equal to the rank at time n. To invoke the transitivity of the ordering on natural numbers one must focus on the three numbers given by the rank of pawn at times n and

```
(IN-CONTEXT ((LET-BE G CHESS-GAME)
            (LET-BE HYP-SATISFIERS
              (THE-SET-OF-ALL
                (LAMBDA ((N NATNUM))
                  (FORALL ((P (WHITE-PAWN-ON-BOARD G N)))
                    (IS (RANK-OF P G N)
                        (GREATER-OR-EQUAL-TO TWO))))))))
            (PUSH-GOAL ;#1
              (IS-EVERY NATURAL-NUMBER
                        (MEMBER-OF HYP-SATISFIERS))))
  (IN-CONTEXT ((PUSH-GOAL ;#2
                (IS ZERO (MEMBER-OF HYP-SATISFIERS))))
    (IN-CONTEXT ((LET-BE ZEROVAR ZERO))
      (IN-CONTEXT ((SUPPOSE
                     (EXISTS-SOME (WHITE-PAWN-ON-BOARD G ZERO)))
                   (LET-BE P (WHITE-PAWN-ON-BOARD G ZERO))
                   (LET-BE TWOVAR TWO))
        (NOTE-GOAL))  ;#2
      (NOTE-GOAL)))  ;#2
  (IN-CONTEXT ((PUSH-GOAL ;#3
                (FORALL ((N (MEMBER-OF HYP-SATISFIERS)))
                  (IS (SUCCESSOR N) (MEMBER-OF HYP-SATISFIERS))))
               (LET-BE SATISFIER (MEMBER-OF HYP-SATISFIERS))
               (LET-BE NEXT-SATISFIER (SUCC SATISFIER)))
    (IN-CONTEXT
        ((PUSH-GOAL ;#4
          (FORALL ((P (WHITE-PAWN-ON-BOARD G NEXT-SATISFIER)))
            (IS (RANK-OF P G NEXT-SATISFIER)
                (GREATER-OR-EQUAL-TO TWO)))))
      (IN-CONTEXT ((SUPPOSE
                     (EXISTS-SOME
                       (WHITE-PAWN-ON-BOARD G NEXT-SATISFIER)))
                   (LET-BE P (WHITE-PAWN-ON-BOARD G NEXT-SATISFIER))
                   (LET-BE R1 (RANK-OF P G SATISFIER))
                   (LET-BE R2 (RANK-OF P G NEXT-SATISFIER))
                   (LET-BE TWOVAR TWO))
        (NOTE-GOAL))  ;#4
      (NOTE-GOAL))  ;#4
    (NOTE-GOAL))  ;#3
  (IN-CONTEXT ((LET-BE N (MEMBER-OF HYP-SATISFIERS)))
    (NOTE (IS HYP-SATISFIERS SET-OF-NATNUM)))
  (NOTE-GOAL))  ;#1
```

Figure 3.3
The proof that white pawns never get to the first rank.

$n + 1$ together with the number two.

The proof shown in figure 3.3 is clearly much longer than a natural
language argument which simply states that white pawns never get to
the first rank. This example indicates that without additional theorem

proving mechanisms the Ontic system will exhibit a large expansion factor on many induction proofs.

One possible mechanism for reducing the expansion factor in induction proofs would be a backward chaining procedure (a tactic) for automatically generating proofs such as the one shown in the figure 3.3. It would be easy to automatically convert the induction hypothesis into a set of numbers and automatically focus on that set of numbers. Furthermore one could automatically attempt to prove the base and induction cases of the argument. As figure 3.3 shows however, proving the base and induction cases with the Ontic system may require focusing on additional objects. In the base case of figure 3.3 the user focuses on an arbitrary white pawn and the number two. In the induction case the user focuses on the rank of the pawn at two different times. It seems that it might be difficult to automatically generate these additional focus objects.

Several automated inference systems include inference mechanisms for handling mathematical induction [BOYR79] [HUET83] [KTNN84]. Research is needed to determine if these, or other, induction mechanisms can be incorporated into the Ontic system. These inference mechanisms are all backward chaining; the induction hypothesis is taken from the goal statement. It would be interesting to see if some forward chaining induction mechanism could be found that was more in the spirit of Ontic's forward chaining inference techniques.

It might be possible to construct a forward chaining induction mechanism as part of Ontic's classification process. Recall that classification involves assigning a set of types to each focus object. Consider a focus object $r(n)$ that involves an arbitrary number n and consider a type τ. It may be possible to prove that the focus object $r(n)$ is an instance of the type τ via induction on the number n. More specifically, the system could show that $r(0)$ is an instance of τ and that if $r(n)$ is an instance of τ then $r(n+1)$ is an instance of τ. In the chess example the focus object $r(n)$ would be (RANK-OF P G N) where P is an arbitrary instance of (WHITE-PAWN-ON-BOARD G N). In the chess example the system would classify the object (RANK-OF P G N) to be an instance of the type (GREATER-OR-EQUAL-TO TWO). This example shows that classification could be made more powerful by incorporating an induction mechanism.

The above examples show that special inference mechanisms for induction are needed in the Ontic system. Hopefully an induction mechanism can be found which allows the above examples to be machine verified at a human, or near-human, level of detail. Similarly, it is hoped that other examples of subhuman system performance will lead to the discovery of more powerful inference mechanisms.

II TECHNICAL DETAILS

4 The Ontic Language

This chapter, and the two that follow, present technical details of the Ontic language and the Ontic theorem proving system. Ontic should be viewed as an object-oriented language and inference system. Intuitively, this means that both the language and the inference process are organized around types and that the inference process is guided by a user-specified set of focus objects. Unfortunately, this high level view of the Ontic language does not specify any of the technical details that must be worked out in building a working system. There are several different kinds of technical details. Some details, such as the organization of the language around type expressions, are fundamental to the object-oriented inference architecture. Other details involve the incorporation of the axioms of Zermelo-Fraenkel set theory. Still other details only improve efficiency or convenience. The presentation of technical details in this chapter and the two that follow emphasize the motivation for each detail.

Some of the features of the Ontic language are similar to features of other well studied higher-order formal languages. More specifically, many formal languages have been proposed in which types can contain free variables, i.e., many formal languages allow *dependent types*. The technical details of syntactic operations on dependent types, such as substitution and β-reduction, have been presented elsewhere [REYN74] [REYN83]. For completeness, however, the details of syntactic operations needed for the implementation of the Ontic system are presented in this chapter.

Although some features of the Ontic language are common to many languages, Ontic's basic object-oriented architecture and Ontic's way of incorporating the axioms of classical set theory appear to be new. More specifically, no previous language has used types as the basis for all predication nor has any previous language represented the axioms of set theory as a simple syntactic reifiability property of higher-order expressions. The inference mechanisms used in Ontic, and discussed in detail in chapters 5 and 6, are also novel.

4.1 The Syntax of Ontic

The expressions in the Ontic language are divided into five kinds: terms, functions, formulas, types and type-generators. In Ontic all predication

is done via types. Each type represents a predicate of one argument
and can be used as such to create atomic formulas of the form (is u τ)
where u is a term and τ is a type. Predicates of more than one argument
are represented by type-generators: operators that take one or more
arguments and return a type. These conventions for predication result
in a large vocabulary of type expressions. This large vocabulary of types
improves both the conciseness of the Ontic language and the efficiency
of the semantic modulation inference mechanism. Ontic appears to be
unique among typed formal languages in that any formula of one free
variable corresponds to a type. The expression of all predication in terms
of types, and the large vocabulary of types that can be achieved with
type-generators, are both central to Ontic's object-oriented architecture.

Formulas, types and type-generators can all be viewed as predicates
that take different numbers of arguments — a formula is a predicate of no
arguments, a type is a predicate of one argument, and a type-generator
is a predicate of more than one argument. However, types are distinguished from formulas and type-generators in that types are intimately
related to variables and quantification. Each Ontic variable is associated with a type and each quantifier ranges over some particular type.
Types are also distinguished from formulas and type-generators by the
role types play in the semantic modulation inference mechanism. The
inference mechanism only references lemmas that quantify over types
that apply to the current focus objects. This insures that lemmas about
topological spaces do not interfere with reasoning about lattices. The
distinction between formulas, types and type-generators is fundamental
to the object-oriented structure of the Ontic system.

The Ontic language can be conceptually divided into three layers corresponding to three languages of increasing complexity. These three
languages will be called quantifier-free Ontic, first-order Ontic, and set-
theoretic Ontic. Quantifier-free Ontic is a syntactic variant of quantifier-
free predicate calculus with equality. Quantifier-free Ontic includes
constant symbols of all five kinds, i.e., terms, functions, types, type-
generators, and formulas. In quantifier-free Ontic all formulas are either proposition symbols, equalities, or formulas of the form (IS s τ)
where s is a term and τ is a type expression. First-order Ontic is a
syntactic variant of first-order predicate calculus. First-order Ontic includes λ-functions, λ-types, λ-type-generators and formulas of the form
(EXISTS-SOME τ) where τ is a type expression. First-order Ontic is

object-oriented: in first-order Ontic types and type-generators are used uniformly instead of predicates; there is a variety of mechanisms for constructing type expressions, and all quantification is typed. Set-theoretic, or full, Ontic is a syntactic variant of Zermelo-Fraenkel set theory. Set-theoretic Ontic includes "reification" expressions described below.

Set-theoretic Ontic is a first-order language in the sense that all quantification is quantification over terms — there is no way of directly quantifying over functions, types, or type-generators. Furthermore, every focus object in an Ontic context must be a term; the Ontic system can not focus on functions, types or type-generators. In Ontic, the distinction between higher-order objects (functions, types, and type-generators) and first-order objects (terms) is used to avoid the paradoxes of set theory. Making set-theoretic Ontic a first-order language provides a direct analogy between set-theoretic Ontic and classical Zermelo-Fraenkel set theory, which is itself a first-order language. The axioms of set theory are organized around the idea that certain higher-order objects can be converted to first-order objects. The process of converting a higher-order object to a first-order object is called *reification*. In order to avoid Russel's paradox the reification process must be carefully controlled. In particular, only "small" higher-order objects can be reified. The Ontic language identifies certain higher-order objects as syntactically small. If f is a syntactically small function expression then (THE-RULE f) is the term which is the reification of f. If τ is a syntactically small type expression then the term (THE-SET-OF-ALL τ) is the reification of τ. Type-generators can be reified indirectly by representing them as functions that return sets. Most of the axioms of set theory are incorporated into the definition of syntactic-smallness for functions, types, and type-generators.

In order for quantifier-free and first-order Ontic to be non-trivial languages, Ontic includes undefined constants. These undefined constants are called "natural kind" constants by analogy with philosophical terminology for undefined terms of natural language [SWRT77]. In set-theoretic Ontic, arbitrary mathematical theorems can be stated and proved without using any natural kind constants. Thus set-theoretic Ontic is foundational in the sense that it allows all mathematics to be built from a small number of primitives, i.e., sets, symbols and rules. In set-theoretic Ontic, natural kind constants should only be used to express statements about undefined terms such as "person". In the formalization of mathematics, natural kind constants should not be used at all.

4.1.1   Terms

Terms are expressions that denote mathematical objects such as sets, pairs, graphs, partially ordered sets and lattices. A term is either a quotation, an application, a variable, or a reification expression. Quotations can be viewed as constant symbols subject to the condition that distinct quotations denote distinct objects. Quotations are not fundamentally necessary but they are tremendously convenient for a host of applications. As in first order predicate calculus, an application term must be the application of a function to the proper number of argument terms.

All variables in the Ontic language are typed — each variable is syntactically associated with a type expression. If x^τ is a variable of type τ, and instances of the type τ exist, then x^τ must denote an instance of the type τ. If there are no instances of the type τ then there are no constraints on the meaning of x^τ. Syntactically typed variables are central to Ontic's object-oriented architecture. The fact that each variable, as a syntactic entity, is associated with a unique type plays an important role in the semantic modulation inference mechanism where variables are analogous to generic individuals in a semantic network. If variables were merely symbols that inherited a type from the context in which they appeared, then one would not be able to view variables as generic individuals in a semantic network. The syntactic association between variables and types also serves the purpose of eliminating any possibility of circularities in the type structure of variables. Conceptually, the existence of a type must precede the existence of any variable of that type. The impossibility of type-circularities simplifies the treatment of λ-expressions of more than one argument.

Reification expressions have already been discussed to some extent. If τ is a syntactically small type then one can construct the reification expression (THE-SET-OF-ALL τ) which denotes the set of instances of the type τ. Smallness is discussed in more detail below. If f is a syntactically small λ-function of one argument then (THE-RULE f) is a term denoting the function f. In principle, the reification operator THE-RULE is redundant with the operator THE-SET-OF-ALL; one could reify a function indirectly by reifying a set of tuples. However, the direct reification of functions is more efficient in two ways. First, the function reification expression is smaller, and thus requires less space to represent and less time to reason about, than the corresponding reification of a set of pairs. Second, the inference rules for function reifications allow proofs to be much shorter than would be possible if reification were restricted to sets. The restriction that one can only reify λ-functions of one argument represents a trade-off between convenience and ease of implementation. This restriction simplifies the control of the inference rules corresponding to the operator THE-RULE at the cost of being forced to reify functions of more than one argument in some indirect manner. This turns out to be a minor inconvenience in practice.

If there is exactly one instance of a type τ then the expression (THE τ) denotes that instances. If there are no instances of τ, or more than one instance, then there are no constraints on the meaning of (THE τ). The operator THE plays two important roles in the Ontic system. First, it is convenient for denoting certain objects. Second, the operator THE plays an important role in incorporating the axioms of set theory. The term (THE τ) is well formed even if τ is not syntactically small. Thus the reification operator THE can be used in cases where THE-SET-OF-ALL can not. This allows for the construction of terms and functions that would not otherwise be expressible. The encoding of the axiom of replacement in the notion of syntactic smallness relies on the fact that a definite expression can be used to specify the value of a λ-function. Although the reification operator THE plays a role in incorporating the axioms of set theory, it does not increase the expressive power of first-order Ontic and thus it is considered to be a first-order feature of the language.

In the following enumeration of Ontic terms those terms that are taken to be part of quantifier-free Ontic are preceded by •, those terms taken to be part of first-order Ontic are preceded by + and those terms in set-theoretic Ontic are preceded by ⋆. The full Ontic language is defined by mutual recursion involving expressions from all three layers.

An Ontic term is any one of the following:

• A natural-kind constant symbol.

• A quotation of the form (QUOTE *symbol*) where *symbol* is an atomic symbol.

• An application of the form $(f\ t_1\ t_2 \ldots t_k)$ where f is a function expression of k arguments and each t_i is a term.

+   A variable x^τ of type τ. We assume that the variables of type
     τ are ordered in an infinite sequence so that we can speak of the
     "first" variable of type τ meeting some condition.

+   An expression of the form (THE τ) where τ is any type expression.

★   A reification term (THE-SET-OF-ALL τ) where τ is a syntactically
     small type expression.

★   A reification term (THE-RULE f) where f is a syntactically small
     λ-function of one argument.

4.1.2   Formulas

A formula is an expression that is either true or false under any particular interpretation of its free variables. An Ontic formula is either
an equality between terms, a Boolean combination of formulas, a is-
formula, or an existence-formula. Equalities and Boolean combinations
have their standard meaning. Existence and is-formulas are fundamental to the object-oriented architecture. In Ontic all predication is done
with is-formulas of the form (IS u τ) where u is a term and τ is a
type. Furthermore, all quantified formulas are existence-formulas of the
form (EXISTS-SOME τ) where τ is a type. Both of these features of
the language are consistent with the view that the language should be
organized around type expressions.

An Ontic formula is any one of the following:

•   A natural kind proposition symbol.

•   An is-formula of the form (IS t τ) where t is a term and τ is a
     type expression.

•   An equality of the form (= e_1 e_2) where e_1 and e_2 are any Ontic
     expressions.

•   A Boolean formula of the form (OR Φ Ψ) or (NOT Φ) where Φ
     and Ψ are formulas.

+   An existence-formula of the form (EXISTS-SOME τ) where τ is a
     type expression.

4.1.3   Functions

The most basic kind of function expression is the λ-function. Ontic λ-functions can have any number of formal arguments. In many languages, such as the pure untyped λ-calculus, functions of more than one argument are represented by Curried functions of one argument. This elimination of λ-expressions of more than one argument theoretically simplifies the language but makes it harder to use in practice; all practical programming languages allow λ-expressions of more than one argument. Furthermore, the ability to Curry functions depends on the existence of higher-order functionals, i.e., expressions that take arguments and return either a function or another higher-order functional, By allowing λ-expressions of more than one argument these higher-order functionals can be eliminated without any significant loss of convenience to the Ontic user. However, λ-expressions of more than one argument introduce the additional conceptual complexity associated with the possibility that one of the formal arguments may appear free in the type of another formal argument. For example, one might define a function N such that the application of N to a graph G and a node x of G returns the set of all immediate neighbors of x in the graph G. In this case the function N takes two arguments where the first must be a graph and the second must be a node in the graph given as a first argument. The type restriction on the second argument depends on the particular value passed as the first argument. We say that the second argument has a *dependent type*. As discussed in the previous section, the fact that the type of a variable must syntactically precede the variable itself insures that there is no danger of circularities in the type structure of variables. Thus there are no λ-functions with circular dependent types.

In addition to λ-functions, the Ontic function expressions include expressions of the form (THE-FUNCTION r) and the primitive function-symbol RULE-DOMAIN. These two additional kinds of function expressions provide a way of converting a reified function, which is a term, back into a function. More specifically, if r is a reified function, and thus a term, the function underlying r can be written as

(LAMBDA $(x$ (MEMBER-OF (RULE-DOMAIN r)))
    ((THE-FUNCTION r) x (MEMBER-OF (RULE-DOMAIN r)))) .

For user-convenience the expression (APPLY r u) can be used as an abbreviation for ((THE-FUNCTION r) u).

Since functions are higher-order objects, i.e., they are not terms or formulas, the Ontic system must identify those function expressions that are syntactically small. Semantically, smallness is determined by the number of tuples in the graph of the function; if we think of a function as a set of tuples then smallness corresponds to the cardinality of the function. A collection has small cardinality if it has fewer members than there are sets in the universe. The axioms of set theory can be viewed as saying that every collection that has small cardinality can be reified and that the universe of all sets has a *very large* cardinality. For a λ-function to have small cardinality it suffices that each domain type has a small cardinality.

An Ontic function is any one of the following:

- A natural-kind function symbol.

+ A λ-function (LAMBDA ($x_1^{\tau_1}$ ... $x_k^{\tau_k}$) u) where each $x_i^{\tau_i}$ is a variable of type τ_i and u is a term. A λ-function is syntactically small just in case each type expression τ_i is syntactically small.

★ An expression of the form (THE-FUNCTION t) where t is a term. Such an expression is a function of one argument and is syntactically small.

★ The primitive function symbol RULE-DOMAIN. This is a function of one argument and is not syntactically small.

4.1.4 Types

There are four primitive types: SYMBOL, SET, RULE and THING. The type SYMBOL corresponds to quotation terms: every quotation term is an instance of the type SYMBOL. The type SET is associated with reified types, every expression of the form (THE-SET-OF-ALL τ) is an instance of the type SET. Similarly, every reified function is an instance of the type RULE. Every term is an instance of the type THING. For definiteness we can assume that every thing is either a symbol, a set, or a rule and the types symbol, set, and rule are disjoint. This assumption is somewhat arbitrary. It is consistent with the inference rules of Ontic to assume that all things are actually sets. It is also consistent to assume that there are things, such as people, that are neither symbols, sets, nor rules. From a pragmatic standpoint, all one really has to know is that quotations are symbols, the reification of a type is a set, the reification of a function is a rule, and every term denotes an instance of the type thing.

As in the case of functions, the smallness of a type is determined by its cardinality. For types this means that a type is small if it has fewer instances than there are sets in the universe. The type SYMBOL is syntactically small since there are fewer quotations than sets. However the types SET, RULE and THING are not small.

In Ontic, a λ-predicate of one argument is a type expression. This allows completely arbitrary predicates to be used as types. An application of a type-generator is also a type. By representing all predicates of more than one argument as type-generators, Ontic allows for a large vocabulary of concise type expressions. Applications of type-generators and λ-types are fundamental to Ontic's object-oriented architecture.

Every instance of a λ-type is also an instance of its domain type, i.e., the type of the formal argument of that λ-type. Thus the number of instances of a λ-type can be no larger than the number of instances of its domain type. A λ-type is classified as syntactically small if its domain type is syntactically small. The smallness of a type-generator is defined differently from the smallness of types and functions. A type-generator is small just in case any application of that type-generator yields a small type. Thus an application of a type-generator is syntactically small just in case the type-generator itself is syntactically small.

If f is a λ-function then the expression (RANGE-TYPE f) is an Ontic type. The type (RANGE-TYPE f) corresponds to the range of the function f: an instance of the type (RANGE-TYPE f) is an object that can be written as $(f\ s_1 \ldots s_n)$ where the arguments $s_1 \ldots s_n$ are instances of the corresponding domain types of f. A type of the form (RANGE-TYPE f) is syntactically small just in case f is syntactically small; if the number of tuples in f has small cardinality then the projection of that set of tuples onto the value component must also have small cardinality. This definition of syntactic smallness for range types yields the set-theoretic axioms of replacement and union. Alternatively, one can view the axioms of replacement and union as embedded in the definition of smallness for λ-functions, but range types are needed before the axioms can be used to construct sets. This encoding of the axiom of replacement relies on the fact that the definite description operator THE can be used to reify sets that are not syntactically small. This encoding of the axiom of union relies on the fact that λ-functions can take more than one argument and that the type of one argument can depend on the value of another. The restriction that RANGE-TYPE can only be applied to λ-functions represents a compromise between expressive convenience and ease of implementation. The restriction simplifies the control of the inference rules associated with RANGE-TYPE and does not seem to cause any significant inconvenience. Although the definition of smallness for expressions of the form (RANGE-TYPE f) plays an important role in the encoding of the axioms of set theory, these expressions are also meaningful and useful in first-order inference. Thus these expressions are included in first-order Ontic.

An Ontic type is any one of the following:

- A natural-kind type symbol.

- The distinguished syntactically small type constant SYMBOL.

- An application of the form $(g \ t_1 \ t_2 \ldots t_k)$ where g is a type-generator of k arguments and each t_i is a term. A type expression of this form is syntactically small just in case the type-generator g is syntactically small.

+ The distinguished syntactically large type constant THING.

+ A λ-type of the form (LAMBDA (x^τ) Φ) where x^τ is a variable of type τ and Φ is a formula. A type of this form is syntactically small just in case the domain type τ is syntactically small.

+ An expression of the form (RANGE-TYPE f) where f is a λ-function of any number of arguments. The type expression (RANGE-TYPE f) is syntactically small just in case the function expression f is syntactically small.

★ One of the distinguished type constants SET and RULE. Both of these types are syntactically large.

4.1.5   Type-Generators

Like λ-functions, λ-type-generators can take any number of arguments and the type of one argument may depend on the value of another argument. Smallness for type-generators is somewhat different from smallness for types or functions. In determining the smallness of a type-generator one is not concerned with the size of the type-generator itself when it is viewed as a set of tuples. Rather, one is concerned with the size of the types that can be generated by applying the type-generator. Thus, a λ-type-generator is syntactically small just in case the body of the λ-type-generator is a syntactically small type.

In addition to λ-type-generators, there are four primitive Ontic type-generators: MEMBER-OF, EITHER, SUBSET-OF, and RULE-BETWEEN. All of these primitive type-generators are syntactically small. The generator MEMBER-OF is the inverse of the set reification operator THE-SET-OF-ALL. Thus, if s is the set resulting from the reification of a type τ, then the type (MEMBER-OF s) is equivalent to the type τ. Thus MEMBER-OF is related to THE-SET-OF-ALL in much the same way that THE-FUNCTION is related to THE-RULE. The instances of types of the form (EITHER u v) consist of exactly the objects denoted by the terms u and v. Semantically, the type-generator EITHER is equivalent to an easily defined λ-expression. However, the λ-expression equivalent to EITHER is syntactically large. The syntactic smallness of the primitive type-generator EITHER incorporates the set-theoretic axiom of pairing. Similar observations hold for the primitives SUBSET-OF and RULE-BETWEEN. Both primitives are semantically equivalent to λ-expressions, but the corresponding λ-expressions would not be syntactically small. The smallness of the primitive SUBSET-OF yields the set-theoretic axiom of power set. The smallness of RULE-BETWEEN incorporates an axiom for rules analogous to the power-set axiom for sets.

An Ontic type-generator is any one of the following:

- A natural-kind type-generator symbol.

+ A λ-type-generator (LAMBDA ($x_1^{\tau_1}$ ... $x_k^{\tau_k}$) σ) where σ is a type expression. A type-generator of this form is syntactically small just in case the type σ is syntactically small.

+ The distinguished syntactically small constant EITHER.

$\star$ One of the constants MEMBER-OF, SUBSET-OF, or RULE-BETWEEN. The type-generator RULE-BETWEEN takes two arguments while the

type-generators MEMBER-OF and SUBSET-OF take one. All these
type-generators are syntactically small.

4.1.6   The Syntactic Classification of Expressions

An Ontic expression is either a term, a formula, a function, a type, or a
type-generator. This classification of expressions is based on the kind of
object an expression denotes, i.e., it is a semantic classification. Ontic
expressions can also be classified in a syntactic way. More specifically,
every Ontic expression is either a constant, a variable, a compositional
application, or a λ-expression.

> **Definition:** An *Ontic constant* is a quotation, a natural-
> kind symbol, or one of the primitive symbols of Ontic.
>
> A *λ-expression* is either a λ-type, a λ-function, or a λ-type-
> generator.
>
> A *compositional application* is any expression other than a
> constant, variable, or λ-expression. All compositional appli-
> cations have the form $(op\ arg_1\ arg_2\ \dots\ arg_k)$.
>
> **Observation:** Every Ontic expression is either a constant,
> a variable, a compositional application, or a λ-expression.

4.1.7   An External Language

Each variable in the Ontic language contains its type as part of its syntax. This feature of the Ontic language is essential for the semantic
modulation inference mechanism described in chapter 6. Unfortunately,
the type expressions associated with variables makes the written form
of Ontic expressions quite long and difficult for users to read and write.
To make expressions easier to read and write, the Ontic implementation communicates with the user in an external language. The external
language is similar to the internal language except that a given variable
in the external language does not have a fixed type. In the external
language a variable inherits its type from the syntactic context in which
it appears. For example, the internal λ-expression (LAMBDA (x^τ) x^τ)
corresponds to the external expression (LAMBDA $((Z\ \tau))$ Z). In the external expression the variable Z is locally associated with the type τ

but the same variable Z might be associated with other types in other contexts.

Although the internal and external languages are quite similar, there are some interesting syntactic differences. Unlike internal variables, external variables inherit their types from the contexts in which they appear. This allows for the possibility of circular type structures. For example, consider an external λ-expression of the form

(LAMBDA ((X (MEMBER-OF Y)) (Y (MEMBER-OF X))) b).

This λ-expression takes two arguments X and Y where X is a member of Y and Y is a member of X. Circularities of this kind can never occur in the internal language. Thus one must explicitly remove all λ-expressions with circular type structures from the external language.

A procedure for translating external expressions into internal expressions is given below. This translation procedure has the property that two external expression that are equivalent up to the renaming of bound variables have the same internal translation. This canonicalization property of the translation process reduces the size of the inference network described in chapter 6.

The translation of external expressions into the internal language is defined relative to a *symbol translation table* which is a partial mapping from external symbols to internal terms. Formally, a translation table is a set of pairs of the form $X \mapsto e$ where X is an external variable e is an (internal) Ontic term and where no external variable is contained in more than one pair. Each context in the Ontic system is associated with a particular symbol translation table. If σ is a type expression in the external language then the context construction operation (LET-BE X σ) constructs a context where the symbol translation table includes the entry $X \mapsto x^{\sigma'}$ where $x^{\sigma'}$ is an internal variable of type σ' and σ' is the internal translation of the external type expression σ. If t is a term in the external language then the context constructor (LET-BE X t) yields a context where the symbol translation table contains the entry $X \mapsto t'$ where t' is the internal translation of the external expression t. New symbol translation tables are also constructed during the translation of external λ-expressions. Consider translating the external expression (LAMBDA ((S SET) (X (MEMBER-OF S))) b) relative to a symbol translation table ρ. To translate this expression one must first construct a new symbol translation table ρ' that both maps the external variable S to an internal variable s^{SET} of type SET and maps the external variable X to an internal variable $x^{(\text{MEMBER-OF } s^{\text{SET}})}$ of type (MEMBER-OF s^{SET}).

The following definition of the translation procedure assumes that the notion of a free variable is well defined on external expressions. Actually, the definition of a free variable is slightly subtle. The definition of a free variable for external expressions corresponds to the definition of a free variable for internal expressions given in section 4.2.1.

> **Definition:** Let e be an external expression and ρ a symbol translation table. The translation $T(e, \rho)$ of the expression e with respect to the table ρ is defined as follows:
>
> - If e is an Ontic constant then $T(e, \rho)$ equals e.
>
> - If e is a variable X of the external language then if ρ contains a pair X $\mapsto t$ then $T(e, \rho)$ equals t, otherwise $T(e, \rho)$ is undefined (an error is generated).
>
> - If e has the form (op arg_1 arg_2 ... arg_k) then $T(e, \rho)$ equals $(T(op, \rho)\ T(arg_1, \rho)\ ...\ T(arg_k, \rho))$.
>
> - If e has the form (LAMBDA ((X_1 τ_1) ... (X_k τ_k)) b) then we must construct a new symbol translation table that translates the external variables X_1 ... X_k. Let *freevars* be the set of all variables that appear free in expressions of the form $\rho(Y)$ where Y is a free variable of e. (This is the set of variables that will appear free in $T(e, \rho)$.) Let *arglist* be the bound variable list ((X_1 τ_1) ... (X_k τ_k)). Finally, let ρ' be the symbol translation table *NewTable*(*arglist*, ρ, *freevars*) where the function *NewTable* is defined below. The translation $T(e, \rho)$ is then defined to be
>
> (LAMBDA $(T(X_1, \rho')\ ...\ T(X_k, \rho'))\ T(b, \rho')$).

NewTable(*arglist*, ρ, *freevars*) is defined as follows:

- If *arglist* is empty then *NewTable*(*arglist*, ρ, *freevars*) equals the table ρ. Otherwise the symbol translation table *NewTable*(*arglist*, ρ, *freevars*) is computed as follows:

- Let $(X_i \; \tau_i)$ be the first pair in *arglist* such that there is no pair $(X_j \; \tau_j)$ in *arglist* such that X_j appears free in τ_i. If no such pair $(X_i \; \tau_i)$ exists then there is a circularity in the type structure of *arglist* and the attempt to construct a new translation table fails.

- If the pair $(X_i \; \tau_i)$ exists let τ_i' be $T(\tau_i, \rho)$ and let $x^{\tau_i'}$ be the first variable of type τ_i' that is not a subvariable[1] of any member of *freevars*.[2]

- Let *restargs* be *arglist* minus $(X_i \; \tau_i)$. Let ρ' be the table that is identical to ρ except that it contains the pair $X_i \mapsto x^{\tau_i'}$ as the mapping of X_i. Let *freevars'* be *freevars* plus x_i^τ and return *NewTable(restargs, ρ', freevars')*.

When selecting an internal variable of type τ we always choose the first variable of type τ that meets an appropriate correctness criterion. This insures that the bound variables in the resulting translation are named in a standard way. Thus external expressions that are equivalent up to the renaming of bound variables translate to the same internal expression.

The translation process used in the Ontic implementation recognizes and expands certain macros. More specifically, the Ontic implementation provides the macros EXISTS, FORALL, IS-EVERY, and EXACTLY-ONE. The expression (EXISTS ((X τ)) Φ) abbreviates the existence formula (EXISTS-SOME (LAMBDA ((X τ)) Φ)) while (FORALL ((X τ)) Φ) abbreviates (NOT (EXISTS ((X τ)) (NOT Φ))). The macros EXISTS and FORALL can also be used to quantify over several variables simultaneously. The expression (IS-EVERY τ σ) abbreviates a formula that says that every instance of τ is an instance of σ. Finally, the expression (EXACTLY-ONE σ) abbreviates a formula that says that there is exactly one instance of the type σ.

The external language also allows for user-specified definitions of the form (DEFINE *symbol e*) where *symbol* is an external symbol and *e* is any external expression. A definition of this form alters the base

---

[1] A variable x^τ is a subvariable of an expression e if either x^τ appears free in e or there is some variable y^σ that appears free in e such that x^τ is a subvariable of the type σ. Free variables and subvariables are discussed in more detail in section 4.2.1.

[2] The definition of the Ontic language states that the variables of any given type τ are ordered in an infinite sequence. Thus we can talk about the "first" variable of type τ satisfying a certain condition.

level symbol translation table so that *symbol* gets translated as the expression e' where e' is the internal translation of e. A mechanism by which the user can define arbitrary additional macros is also provided, although users are strongly encouraged to use definitions rather than macros whenever possible. In practice, very few additional macros are ever defined.

4.2   Well-Formedness and Substitution

This section presents definitions and syntactic procedures that apply to any language with dependent types, i.e., types that contain free variables. Since dependent types are a common feature of well-studied languages, details of syntactic operations in the presence of such types have been worked out by other authors [REYN74] [REYN83]. However, the details presented below are particularly well-suited to the Ontic language and provide a complete specification for a set of syntactic operations sufficient for implementing Ontic.

4.2.1   Free Variables and Subvariables

In computing the set of free variables of an Ontic expression one must properly handle the types of bound variables. Consider a λ-expression of the form (LAMBDA $(x_1^{\tau_1} \ \ldots \ x_k^{\tau_k})$ b). If this λ-expression is a λ-type then it denotes the class of instances of that type. If the λ-expression is a function or type-generator then it denotes a certain class of tuples. In either case, the meaning of the λ-expression depends on the classes associated with the types τ_i which in turn can depend on the interpretation of free variables in the type expressions. Thus the free variables of a λ-expression should include free variables in the types of the bound parameters. However, a free variable of a type τ_i that also appears in the parameter list as another bound variable $x_j^{\tau_j}$ is considered to be bound in τ_i and is not included in the free variables of the λ-expression. Thus the type of one argument may depend on the value of another argument; this is the essence of dependent types. The fact that the type of each variable is syntactically prior to the variable itself insures that there can be no circularities in the dependencies between the arguments of a λ-expression.

In languages with dependent types it is possible to distinguish two kinds of free variable. I will use the terms "free variable" and "subvariable". The distinction between free variables and subvariables can be initially motivated by the idea that the meaning of an expression is completely determined by the meaning of its free variables while the subvariables of an expression include both the free variables and variables that influence the types of the free variables. Other presentations of languages with dependent types do not distinguish between free variables and subvariables. However, the distinction between free variables and subvariables seems semantically well-motivated and plays a significant role in efficiently implementing the semantic-modulation version of the universal generalization rule as described in chapter 6.

Definition: A variable y^σ is a *free variable* of an expression e if one of the following conditions hold:

- e is the variable y^σ.
- e is an application ($op\ arg_1\ arg_2\ \ldots\ arg_k$) and y^σ is a free variable of the operator op or one of the arguments arg_i.
- e is a λ-expression (LAMBDA ($x_1^{\tau_1}\ \ldots\ x_k^{\tau_k}$) b), y^σ is a free variable of either the body b or one of the types τ_i, and y^σ is distinct from each of the bound variables $x_i^{\tau_i}$.

Consider two variables x^τ and y^σ such that x^τ appears free in the type σ. According to the definition above, the variable x^τ does not appear free in the variable y^σ; the variable y^σ has no free variables other than itself. However, the variable x^τ is clearly related in some way to the variable y^σ; changing the semantic interpretation of x^τ changes the interpretation of the type of y^σ. We say that x^τ is a *subvariable* of y^σ.

Definition: A variable x^τ is a *subvariable* of an expression u if either x^τ is a free variable of u or there exists some free variable y^σ of u such that x^τ is a subvariable of the type σ of y^σ.

4.2.2 Well-Formedness

The (internal) Ontic language defined above includes certain expressions whose semantic interpretation is problematic. Consider the function

(LAMBDA (x^{NUMBER}) (+ x^{NUMBER} $y^{(\text{GREATER-THAN } x^{\text{NUMBER}})}$)).

Note that this function has the form (LAMBDA (x^τ) (+ x^τ y^σ)) where x^τ appears free in the type σ. Let f denote this λ-function and consider an application of f, such as the expression (f 3). Since σ is the type (greater-than x^τ), the variable y^σ appears to be constrained to always be larger than x^τ. Thus we would expect that (f 3) must be at least 7, and in general one would expect that (f n) must be greater than $2n$. However, the value of (f u) seems to be undetermined since y^σ can be any number greater than the argument x^τ. If x^τ did not appear free in the type σ then the meaning of f is clear. More specifically, if x^τ did not appear free in σ then y^σ can simply be treated as a free variable of f. The semantic meaning of an expression is always defined relative to some variable interpretation that assigns values to the free variables of the expression. If y^σ is simply treated as a free variable of f, then f would denote the function that added the fixed value of y^σ to whatever argument it is given. However, if the type σ contains the argument x^τ as a free variable then the meaning of f is not clear.

There are two possible solutions to this difficulty. First, one can adopt conventions that assign unambiguous meanings to these problematic expressions. One must then insure that syntactic operations, such as β-conversion, are consistent with these adopted conventions (β-conversion should preserve the meaning of an expression). The second option is to simply eliminate the problematic expressions from the language. The second option is taken here: the class of problematic expressions is syntactically identified as ill-formed and eliminated from the language. However, the first option, that of assigning meaning to the problematic expressions, is also a reasonable approach and deserves some comment.

Let f be a λ-expression of the form (LAMBDA (x^τ) (g x^τ y^σ)) where x^τ appears free in the type σ. This expression can be assigned a meaning by forcing y^σ to be treated as a free variable. In this case the occurrence of x^τ in the type σ is not captured by the formal parameter of the λ-expression. Under this semantic treatment (LAMBDA (x^τ) (g x^τ y^σ)) is α-equivalent to the expression (LAMBDA (z^τ) (g z^τ y^σ)) where z^τ does not appear free in σ. To make β-conversion consistent with this semantic convention one must define syntactic substitution carefully. In particular, suppose that ω is a syntactic substitution, i.e. a mapping from variables to terms. If y^σ is not mapped by the substitution ω then

$\omega(y^\sigma)$ should be defined to be y^σ rather than some variable of type $\omega(\sigma)$, i.e. syntactic substitution on a variable should not induce a substitution on the type of the variable. This simple convention for syntactic substitution yields syntactic operations that are consistent with the above semantic conventions for problematic expressions. Unfortunately, this convention for syntactic substitution leads to difficulties in the presentation of the semantic modulation inference mechanism in chapter 6. The possible alternative definitions of substitution and their relationship to problematic expressions are discussed further in section 4.2.3.

> **Definition:** A λ-expression (LAMBDA $(x_1^{T_1} \ \ldots \ x_k^{T_k})$ b) is called *ill-formed* if there is some free variable y^σ of the λ-expression such that one of the bound parameters $x_i^{T_i}$ is a subvariable of the type σ.

The λ-expression

(LAMBDA (x^{NUMBER}) $(+ \ x^{\text{NUMBER}} \ y^{(\text{GREATER-THAN} \ x^{\text{NUMBER}})}))$

is ill-formed because the bound variable x^{NUMBER} is a subvariable of the type of the free variable $y^{(\text{GREATER-THAN} \ x^{\text{NUMBER}})}$.

4.2.3   Substitution

A syntactic substitution is a finite map from variables to terms.

> **Definition:** A *syntactic substitution* is a partial mapping from variables to terms. More specifically, a syntactic substitution is a set ω of pairs of the form $y^\sigma \mapsto t$ where y^σ is a variable and t is a term and a given variable appears as the left hand side of at most one pair in ω. A variable y^σ is directly mapped by ω if ω contains a pair of the form $y^\sigma \mapsto t$.

We write $\omega(e)$ to denote the result of applying the syntactic substitution ω to the expression e. There are two different definitions of the result of applying a substitution that both appear sensible. The two definitions differ on the value of $\omega(y^\sigma)$ in the case where y^σ is a variable that is not directly mapped ω. Under the first definition, which I will call simple substitution, if y^σ is not directly mapped by ω then $\omega(y^\sigma)$

equals y^σ. Under the second definition, which I will call sophisticated substitution, if y^σ is not directly mapped by ω then $\omega(y^\sigma)$ is guaranteed to be a variable of type $\omega(\sigma)$: if $\omega(\sigma)$ equals σ then $\omega(y^\sigma)$ equals y^σ, but if $\omega(\sigma)$ does not equal σ then $\omega(y^\sigma)$ is some variable of type $\omega(\sigma)$. The method of choosing a variable of type $\omega(\sigma)$ is discussed below.

Both simple and sophisticated substitution are sensible. More specifically, in the Ontic implementation syntactic substitution is only used in one place: to compute β-reductions of applications of λ-expressions. Furthermore, one can show that in the β-reduction of well-formed (non-problematic) expressions, simplified substitution and sophisticated substitution produce the same result.[3] More specifically, during the β-conversion of well-formed expressions the recursive substitution procedure maintains the invariant that if y^σ is a free variable of e, and y^σ is not directly mapped by ω, then no subvariable of the type σ is mapped by ω. In this case $\omega(y^\sigma)$ equals y^σ under both versions of substitution.

When ill-formed expressions are allowed, the two versions of substitution produce different results. The simplified version produces a result consistent with the semantics of ill-formed expressions defined above. The "sophisticated" version produces a result that does not seem consistent with any sensible semantics of application. Thus simple substitution would seem superior in all respects; it is easier to compute and, unlike sophisticated substitution, it can be used to correctly compute β-conversions on ill-formed expressions. However, sophisticated substitution is more convenient in the theoretical description of semantic modulation presented in chapter 6. Semantic modulation uses a combination of "binding" and congruence closure to simulate the application of a syntactic substitution to the entire data base. It turns out that semantic modulation simulates sophisticated, rather than simple, substitution. Thus, to simplify the discussion of semantic modulation, we restrict our attention to sophisticated substitution.

There is a technical difficulty in sophisticated substitution involving the selection of a variable of a given type. Suppose y^σ is not directly mapped by ω but that $\omega(\sigma)$ is not equal to σ. In this case, under sophisticated substitution, $\omega(y^\sigma)$ is a variable of type $\omega(\sigma)$. The following definition sets $\omega(y^\sigma)$ equals to the variable $\lceil y\text{-}\sigma \rceil^{\omega(\sigma)}$ of type $\omega(\sigma)$ where $\lceil y\text{-}\sigma \rceil$ is a new token unique to the variable y^σ. The definition of the

---

[3] Because the two versions produce the same result in all cases where substitution is used in the implementation, only simple substitution need be implemented.

Ontic language specifies that the variables of a given type τ are ordered so that one can refer to the first variable of type τ, the second variable of type τ, and so on. A variable of the form $\lceil y\text{-}\sigma \rceil^\tau$ has an infinite index in this sequence. Thus, a variable of the form $\lceil y\text{-}\sigma \rceil^{\omega(\sigma)}$ is "new" in the sense that it is never generated during the translation of external expressions into the internal language or in the β-reduction of internal expressions that do not already contain such variables. In fact, variables of this form do not need to be implemented at all; sophisticated substitution is only needed as a conceptual tool in understanding semantic modulation.

As in all languages with quantifiers, the substitution procedure must rename bound variables. In Ontic this renaming serves three purposes. First, as in other languages, the renaming of bound variables avoids the capture of free variables introduced by the substitution. Second, because substitution may change the type of a bound variable, the substitution must often replace a bound variable of one type with a bound variable of a different type. Finally, by standardizing the naming of bound variables we avoid constructing distinct expressions that differ only in the naming of bound variables.

Definition: For any syntactic substitution ω and any Ontic expression e, the expression $\omega(e)$ is defined as follows:

- If no subvariable of e is mapped by ω then $\omega(e)$ equals e.

- If e is a variable y^σ such that ω contains a pair $y^\sigma \mapsto t$ then $\omega(e)$ equals t.

- If e is a variable y^σ not mapped by ω, but some subvariable of the type σ is mapped by ω, then $\omega(e)$ is the variable $\lceil y\text{-}\sigma \rceil^{\omega(\sigma)}$ where $\lceil y\text{-}\sigma \rceil$ is a token unique to the variable y^σ and of infinite index in the sequence of variables of type $\omega(\sigma)$.

- If e has the form $(op\ arg_1\ arg_2\ \ldots\ arg_k)$ then $\omega(e)$ is the expression $(\omega(op)\ \omega(arg_1)\ \omega(arg_2)\ \ldots\ \omega(arg_k))$

- If e is a λ-expression (LAMBDA $(x_1^{\tau_1}\ \ldots\ x_k^{\tau_k})\ b)$ then let *freevars* be the set of variables that occur free in an

expression of the form $\omega(y^\sigma)$ where y^σ is a free variable
of e. (The set *freevars* contains those variables that
will appear free in the expression $\omega(e)$.) Let *arglist* be
the list of variables $(x_1^{\tau_1} \ \ldots \ x_k^{\tau_k})$ and let ω' be the variable substitution *Rename*(*arglist*, ω, *freevars*) where the
function *Rename* is defined below. In this case $\omega(e)$
equals (LAMBDA $(\omega'(x_1^{\tau_1}) \ \ldots \omega'(x_k^{\tau_k}))$ $\omega'(b))$

Rename(*arglist*, ω, *freevars*) is defined as follows:

- If the parameter list *arglist* is empty then the substitution *Rename*(*arglist*, ω, *freevars*) equals the substitution ω. Otherwise *Rename*(*arglist*, ω, *freevars*) is computed as follows:

- Let $x_i^{\tau_i}$ be the first member of the argument list such
  that no variable $x_j^{\tau_j}$ in the argument list appears free
  in τ_i. Such an argument must exist because no list of
  Ontic variables can have circular types.

- Let $z^{\omega(\tau_i)}$ be the first variable of type $\omega(\tau_i)$ such that
  $z^{\omega(\tau_i)}$ is not a subvariable of a member of *freevars*.

- Let *restargs* be *arglist* minus the argument $x_i^{\tau_i}$.

- Let ω' be the substitution that is identical to ω except
  that it contains the pair $x_i^{\tau_i} \mapsto z^{\omega(\tau_i)}$ as the mapping of
  $x_i^{\tau_i}$.

- Let *freevars'* be *freevars* plus the variable $z^{\omega(\tau_i)}$.

- Return *Rename*(*restargs*, ω', *freevars'*).

The function *Rename* always renames a variable x^τ to be the first
variable of type $\omega(\tau)$ that satisfies a certain correctness criterion. This
has the effect of standardizing the naming of bound variables. In fact,
for any substitution ω, if two expressions e and e' are identical up to the
renaming of bound variables then $\omega(e_1)$ is the same expression as $\omega(e_2)$.

4.3 Congruence Combinators

The congruence inference rule allows for the substitution of equals for equals. Unfortunately, unrestricted substitution into the scope of quantifiers is not logically sound; if we are told that x^τ equals 3 we can not conclude that (LAMBDA (x^τ) $(f\ x^\tau)$) equals (LAMBDA (x^τ) $(f\ 3)$). Technically, substitution of equals for equals inside the scope of quantifiers is not necessary — any equation between terms that is provable using sound substitutions inside the scope of quantifiers can be proven, with perhaps a longer proof, without resorting to substitution inside the scope of quantifiers. However, proof length can be reduced by allowing certain substitutions into the scope of quantifiers. One approach to substitution inside the scope of quantifiers is based on de Bruijn notation [DBRJ72]. In de Bruijn notation bound variables are represented by special tokens called deBruijn numbers. In a de Bruijn notation approach to the substitution problem one could ensure that deBruijn numbers never appear free in the internal translations of external expressions. This would, in turn, ensure that the substitution of equals for equals inside the scope of quantifiers was sound. A second approach to substitution inside the scope of quantifiers, and the one adopted in the Ontic implementation, is based on representing λ-expressions in terms of *congruence combinators*. More specifically, the congruence combinator representation of a λ-expression is an application of the form $(K\ u_1 \ldots u_n)$ where K is a congruence combinator and $u_1 \ldots u_n$ are the "maximal free subexpressions" of the original λ-expression. The congruence combinator can be represented by any data structure that satisfies two properties. First, it must allow the original λ-expression to be reconstructed, at least in principle, from the congruence combinator representation. Second, any two λ-expressions that are "identical up to the replacement of free subexpressions" should have the same congruence combinator.

First, we define a general notion of a position. To formally define a position one can think of an expression as a tree. A position in a tree can be specified by a sequence of numbers. For example the sequence <2, 1, 3> specifies the position arrived at by starting at the root, taking the second top level subexpression, then taking the first subexpression of that, and finally, taking the third subexpression of the result. For example, if e is the expression $(f\ ((g\ a\ b)\ c))$, then the position <2, 1, 3> is occupied by the expression b in the expression e. In general a position is a sequence of numbers specifying a subexpression. If p is a position and e is an expression then the notion $p[e]$ will be used to represent the expression that occupies position p in expression e. A given position p need not be occupied in a given expression e. For example, the position $<2, 3>$ is not occupied in the expression $(f\ ((g\ a\ b)\ c))$. If p is not occupied in e then $p[e]$ is undefined.

The empty sequence of natural numbers will be called the *root position* and if p is the root position then for any expression e, $p[e]$ equals e. A sequence containing exactly one number will be called a *top level* position. If p is a top level position, and p is occupied in e, then $p[e]$ is called a *top level subexpression* of e. There is a natural containment relation between positions. Consider two positions p and q. If the sequence p is a proper extension of the sequence q then we say that position p is *below* q, or that q is *above* p. If position p is below position q, and both p and q are occupied in e, then $p[e]$ is a subexpression of $q[e]$. The root position is above all other positions and every non-root position is either a top level position or is below exactly one top level position.

Constants do not have any top level subexpressions: if p is a position other than the root position, and c is a constant, then p is not occupied in c. The top level subexpressions of a compositional application of the form $(h\ e_1\ \ldots\ e_n)$ are the expressions $h, e_1, \ldots e_n$. A variable x^τ has one top level subexpression which is the type τ. The top level subexpressions of a λ-expression $(\text{LAMBDA}\ (x_1^{\tau_1}\ \ldots\ x_k^{\tau_k})\ b)$ are the variables $(x_1^{\tau_1}\ \ldots\ x_k^{\tau_k})$ and the body b.

Now we consider the notion of a *free* position. Intuitively, a free position in an expression is a location in that expression where the substitution of equals for equals can be done safely. Substitution into the type of a variable results in a new variable even if the new type is equivalent to the old type. In this case the meaning of the new variable is not constrained to be the same as the meaning of the old variable. Thus substitution of equals for equals into the type of a variable does not preserve meaning. However, substitution into the type of an argument of a λ-expression can be done in a way that preserves meaning. If σ and τ are equivalent types then $(\text{LAMBDA}\ (x^\tau)\ (f\ x^\tau))$ is semantically equivalent to $(\text{LAMBDA}\ (x^\sigma)\ (f\ x^\sigma))$. Thus the type of an argument to a λ-expression can correspond to a free position. The definition of a free position identifies those positions at which substitution can be done safely.

Definition: Let e be an expression. If q is a position such
that $q[e]$ is a λ-expression then the positions below q that correspond to the formal arguments of $q[e]$ are called *argument
positions* in e. For example, <1, 2> is an argument position
in the compositional application $((\text{LAMBDA } (x^\tau \ y^\sigma) \ b) \ s)$.

A *variable position* in e is a position p, other than an argument position in e, such that $p[e]$ is a variable.

A position that is under a variable position in e is said to be
variable-covered in e.

A position p is said to be λ-*covered* in e if there exists a
position q above p such that $q[e]$ is a λ-expression and some
variable in the parameter list of $q[e]$ is a free variable of $p[e]$.

A position p is *free* in e if it is occupied in e and is neither
variable-covered nor λ-covered in e.

Intuitively, the substitution of equals for equals can be done inside the
scope of a quantifier as long as the substitution is done at free positions.
In building a congruence combinator representation of a λ-expression
one is concerned with only the maximal internal free positions.

Definition A *maximal internal free position* of an expression
e is a non-root position p that is free in e and is not below
any other non-root free position in e.

Consider a λ-expression with congruence combinator representation
$(K \ u_1 \ \dots \ u_n)$. The congruence combinator representation has the
property that the expressions $u_1, \dots u_n$ are in one to one correspondence
with the maximal internal free positions of the represented λ-expression.
As stated above, the congruence combinator K can be represented by
any data structure satisfying two conditions. First, the data structure
for K must allow, at least in principle, the reconstruction of the λ-
expression from its congruence combinator representation. Second, the
congruence combinator data structure must be sufficiently abstract so
that if a λ-expression s can be converted to a λ-expression t by a series
of substitutions at free positions and renamings of bound variables, then
the congruence combinator used in the representation of s must be the
same as the congruence combinator used in the representation of t.

It turns out that the congruence combinator associated with a λ-expression s can be represented by a λ-expressions with "holes" or "slots" at the maximal free positions. The λ-expression representing the congruence combinator associated with s is isomorphic to a certain root fragment of the expression s itself. The expression that represents the congruence combinator associated with a λ-expression s will be called the *root-syntax combinator* for s. The root-syntax combinator of a λ-expression s is the result of inserting a hole, represented by the token ?, at each maximal free position of s. Consider the λ-expression (LAMBDA (x^τ) $(f$ $x^\tau)$) where f is a function expression that does not contain any free occurrences of x^τ. This expression has two maximal free positions, one occupied by the type expression τ in the parameter list and one occupied by the function expression f. In computing the root syntax of this expression, the type τ and the function f are replaced by ?. This requires replacing the variable x^τ with a variable whose type expression is the token ?. The root syntax of this expression is an expression of the form (LAMBDA $(y^?)$ $(?$ $y^?)$). Although it appears that this expression has three holes, represented by occurrences of ?, only two of these holes correspond to free positions: the third hole occurs at a variable-covered position.

The root-syntax representation of congruence combinators prevents common subexpression optimizations. Consider a λ-expression with two maximal internal free positions and with congruence combinator representation $(K$ s $s)$. In this case the two maximal free positions are occupied by the same expression. In this case one might think that a "more efficient" combinator representation could be achieved via common subexpression optimization: one could use a representation of the form $(K'$ $s)$ where K' is a different combinator. However, this is not possible when using root-syntax combinators. This avoidance of common subexpression optimizations is necessary if one intends to use congruence combinator representations as a basis for congruence inferences, i.e., inferences involving the substitution of equals for equals. Consider the λ-expression mentioned above with congruence combinator representation $(K$ s $s)$. Now consider another λ-expression, identical to the first except that the second maximal internal free subexpression has been replaced by a different, but equivalent, expression t. The congruence combinator representation of this second λ-expression is $(K$ s $t)$. Now if s can be proven equal to t then the congruence inference rule can be used to prove that $(K\ s\ s)$ equals $(K\ s\ t)$. However, if the first λ-expression had been represented as $(K'\ s)$ then the congruence inference rule could not be applied to prove that the two combinator representations are equal. For this reason, common subexpression optimization is not done. The following definition gives a way of computing the root-syntax combinator for a λ-expression.

Definition: Let s be an arbitrary λ-expression of the form $(\texttt{LAMBDA}\ (x_1^{\tau_1}\ \dots\ x_k^{\tau_k})\ b)$. Let $arglist$ be the argument list $(x_1^{\tau_1}\ \dots\ x_k^{\tau_k})$, let γ be the empty variable substitution, and let $freevars$ be the empty list of variables. Let ω be the substitution $RRename(arglist, \gamma, freevars)$ where the function $RRename$ is defined below. The root-syntax combinator of e is defined to be the expression

$$(\texttt{LAMBDA}\ (\omega(x_1^{\tau_1})\dots\omega(x_n^{\tau_n}))\ RSyntax(b, \omega))$$

where the function $RSyntax$ is defined below.

$RRename(arglist, \omega, freevars)$ is defined as follows:

- If $arglist$ is empty then $RRename(arglist, \omega, freevars)$ equals ω. Otherwise $RRename(arglist, \omega, freevars)$ is computed as follows:

- Let $x_i^{\tau_i}$ be the first member of the argument list such that no variable $x_j^{\tau_j}$ in the argument list appears free in τ_i. Such an argument must exist because no list of Ontic variables can have circular types.

- Let τ_i' be the type $RSyntax(\tau_i, \omega)$. Let $z^{\tau_i'}$ be the first variable of type τ_i' such that $z^{\tau_i'}$ is not a subvariable of a member of $freevars$.

- Let $restargs$ be $arglist$ minus $x_i^{\tau_i}$. Let ω' be the substitution that is identical to ω except that it contains the additional pair $x_i^{\tau_i} \mapsto z^{\tau'}$ as the mapping of $x_i^{\tau_i}$. Let $freevars'$ be $freevars$ plus the variable $z^{\tau_i'}$ and return the substitution $RRename(restargs, \omega', freevars')$

$RSyntax(e, \omega)$ is defined as follows:

- If no free variable of e is mapped by the substitution ω then $RSyntax(e, \omega)$ is the token "?".

- If e is a variable mapped by ω then $RSyntax(e, \omega)$ equals $\omega(e)$.

- If e is a compositional application $(f\ u_1\ \ldots\ u_k)$ then $RSyntax(e, \omega)$ equals

  $(RSyntax(f, \omega)\ RSyntax(u_1, \omega)\ \ldots\ RSyntax(u_k, \omega))$.

- If e is a λ-expression (LAMBDA $(x_1^{\tau_1}\ \ldots\ x_k^{\tau_k})$ b) then let *freevars* be those variables that can be written as $\omega(y^\sigma)$ where y^σ is a free variable of e that is mapped by ω. Let ω' be $RRename((x_1^{\tau_1}\ \ldots\ x_k^{\tau_k}), \omega, freevars)$. In this case $RSyntax(e, \omega)$ equals

  (LAMBDA $(\omega'(x_1^{\tau_1})\ \ldots \omega'(x_k^{\tau_k}))$ $RSyntax(b, \omega'))$.

The Ontic language has now been precisely defined and procedures for syntactic manipulation have been given in detail. Chapter 5 specifies the Ontic verification system in terms of inference rules and chapter 6 discusses the implementation of a verification system built on those rules. It is hoped that these details, together with those in the following chapters, will allow other researchers to build their own Ontic systems.

5 Rules of Inference

The Ontic verification system is based on the concept of a high-level proof language. Intuitively, a high-level proof can be viewed as a series of statements where each statement "obviously" follows from previously proven lemmas and earlier steps in the proof. This chapter defines a technical notion of obviousness in terms of incomplete inference rules called rules of obviousness. Each rule of obviousness states that if certain antecedent facts are obvious then a certain conclusion is also obvious. The term obvious is being used in a technical sense; there is no necessary relationship between the technical notion of obvious defined by a set of rules of obviousness and the notion of obvious that can be empirically observed in natural mathematical arguments. The rules of obviousness presented in this chapter are motivated by the desire to make the notion of obvious as powerful as possible under the constraint that one can construct an algorithm for quickly determining whether or not a given statement is obvious.

The rules of obviousness must be carefully crafted to be both powerful and quickly decidable in the sense that some algorithm can quickly determine whether or not there exists a derivation of a given formula using the rules of obviousness. Since logical entailment is undecidable for any language as strong as first order logic, the rules of obviousness must be incomplete, i.e., there must exist mathematical statements that are provable from the axioms of set theory but are not obvious. However, it is possible to craft a set of rules of obviousness such that the high-level proof system based on the notion of obvious derived from those rules is quite powerful, i.e., proofs in that high-level system are short. Ultimately, the power of a given set of inference rules must be determined empirically by measuring the lengths of proofs written in a high-level language based on those rules.

The particular rules of obviousness that are used to specify the Ontic system involve the notion of focus objects. Each step in an Ontic high-level proof is embedded in a context that specifies both a set of suppositions and a set of focus objects. Certain rules of obviousness only apply to focus objects. If these focus-restricted rules of inference were left unrestricted, the resulting notion of obvious would be undecidable. Thus focus objects play a central role in the construction a notion of obvious that is both powerful and quickly decidable.

Unfortunately, the Ontic implementation only approximates the notion of obvious specified by the rules of obviousness given in this chapter. More specifically, it is possible to construct situations in which a statement that is derivable under the rules of obviousness is not, in fact, obvious to the Ontic implementation. Thus, one might say that the Ontic implementation is incomplete relative to the rules of obviousness given in this chapter. Examples of the incompleteness of the implementation seem to be rare; no such incompleteness was encountered in the proof of the Stone Representation theorem. The reasons for the technical incompleteness of the implementation relative to the rules of obviousness are discussed in chapter 6. In practice one can assume that a statement is obvious if and only if it can be derived from the rules of obviousness.

The symbol $\vdash\!\circ$ will be used to denote the inference relation generated by the rules of obviousness. The notation $\Gamma, \mathcal{F} \vdash\!\circ \Phi$ means that the formula Φ can be derived from the set of formulas Γ under focus set $\mathcal{F}$ using the rules of obviousness, i.e., Φ obviously follows from Γ. The high-level proof language corresponds to a different inference relation: the traditional inference symbol $\vdash$ will be used to denote the relation corresponding to the high-level proof system. The notation $\Gamma \vdash \Phi$ means that there exists a high-level proof of Φ from the assumptions in Γ. The following sections list the rules of obviousnesness, specify the high-level proof language, and define correctness for high-level proofs in terms of the notion of obvious encoded in the rules of obviousness. The rules of obviousness involve a special token **FALSE** that represents falsehood. We write $\Gamma, \mathcal{F} \vdash\!\circ$ **FALSE** to indicate that the assumptions in Γ obviously lead to a contradiction under the focus set $\mathcal{F}$.

The Ontic language consists of three layers: quantifier-free Ontic, first-order Ontic, and set-theoretic Ontic. The presentation of Ontic's rules of obviousness is organized around these three layers of the Ontic language. Within each layer the rules are organized around particular kinds of expressions — each kind of Ontic expression is associated with a set of rules that implicitly give the meaning of expressions of that kind. Certain classes of Ontic expressions are associated with both rules of obviousness and *auxiliary formulas*. Auxiliary formulas play an important role in the specification of the network generation mechanism given in section 6.3 but are defined on a case by case basis along with the rules of obviousness.

5.1 Quantifier-Free Rules

The most basic rules of obviousness involve Boolean connectives, equality, and quotations. These rules are collectively called the quantifier-free rules of obviousness. Ontic's Boolean constraint propagation and congruence closure inference mechanisms provide a polynomial time decision procedure for the notion of obviousness generated by the quantifier-free rules. Since a polynomial time decision procedure exists for the quantifier-free rules, and since quantifier-free Ontic can express arbitrary Boolean formulas, it is not surprising that these rules are not semantically complete for quantifier-free Ontic. Intuitively, the rules of obviousness do not provide any mechanism for reasoning by case analysis. However, case analysis is a fundamental feature of the high-level proof language and any valid formula of quantifier-free predicate calculus can be proven using the high-level proof system.

The quantifier-free rules do not involve the focus set $\mathcal{F}$. In presenting the quantifier-free rules, the notation $\Gamma \vdash \Phi$ will be used as an abbreviation for $\Gamma, \mathcal{F} \vdash \Phi$ where $\mathcal{F}$ is an arbitrary focus set.

The first collection of rules of obviousness involves fundamental properties of the obviousness relation $\vdash$ and Boolean connectives. In defining the Ontic language the operations OR and NOT were taken to be the primitive Boolean operators. Other standard Boolean operations such as conjunction and implication are treated in the standard way as abbreviations for expressions involving OR and NOT.

Boolean Connectives:

- If Ψ is a member of Γ then $\Gamma \vdash \Psi$.
- If $\Gamma \vdash$ (NOT (NOT Φ)) then $\Gamma \vdash \Phi$.
- If $\Gamma \vdash \Phi$ then $\Gamma \vdash$ (NOT (NOT Φ)).
- If $\Gamma \vdash \Phi$ and $\Gamma \vdash$ (NOT Φ) then $\Gamma \vdash$ **FALSE**.
- If $\Gamma \vdash$ (NOT Ψ) and $\Gamma \vdash$ (OR Ψ Φ) then $\Gamma \vdash \Phi$.
- If $\Gamma \vdash$ (NOT Φ) and $\Gamma \vdash$ (OR Ψ Φ) then $\Gamma \vdash \Psi$.
- If $\Gamma \vdash$ (NOT (OR Ψ Φ)) then $\Gamma \vdash$ (NOT Φ).
- If $\Gamma \vdash$ (NOT (OR Ψ Φ)) then $\Gamma \vdash$ (NOT Ψ).

- If $\Gamma \vdash\!\!\circ \Psi$ then $\Gamma \vdash\!\!\circ$ (OR Ψ Φ).
- If $\Gamma \vdash\!\!\circ \Phi$ then $\Gamma \vdash\!\!\circ$ (OR Ψ Φ).
- If $\Gamma \vdash\!\!\circ$ (NOT Ψ) and $\Gamma \vdash\!\!\circ$ (NOT Φ) then $\Gamma \vdash\!\!\circ$ (NOT (OR Ψ Φ)).

The formula (IMPLIES Φ Ψ) can be viewed as an abbreviation for (OR (NOT Φ) Ψ). Using this abbreviation convention, the inference rules above imply that if $\Gamma \vdash\!\!\circ$ (IMPLIES Φ Ψ) and $\Gamma \vdash\!\!\circ \Phi$ then $\Gamma \vdash\!\!\circ \Psi$. Similarly, if $\Gamma \vdash\!\!\circ$ (IMPLIES Φ Ψ) and $\Gamma \vdash\!\!\circ$ (NOT Ψ) then $\Gamma \vdash\!\!\circ$ (NOT Φ). Many other inference rules can be derived from the above rules when other Boolean connectives are treated as standard abbreviations for expressions involving OR and NOT. Each non-atomic formula in an assumption set Γ can be viewed as a local constraint on the truth value of the formulas it contains. In certain cases the Boolean rules of obviousness can be used to derive long chains of "constraint propagation" inferences. In fact, the Boolean rules of obviousness are designed to model the Boolean constraint propagation inference mechanism in the Ontic implementation.

The Boolean rules of obviousness are not complete for Boolean logic. In particular suppose Γ consists of the two statements (IMPLIES Φ Ψ) and (IMPLIES Φ (NOT Ψ)). In this case the formula (NOT Φ) semantically follows from Γ. However, it is possible to show that the above rules of inference fail to derive (NOT Φ) from these premises. The Boolean rules of obviousness could be made complete via the addition of an inference rule for refutation.

Refutation:

- If $\Gamma \cup \{\Phi\} \vdash \Psi$ and $\Gamma \cup \{\Phi\} \vdash$ (NOT Ψ) then $\Gamma \vdash$ (NOT Φ).

The above rule of refutation is *not* a rule of obviousness. If this rule were included in the rules of obviousness then deciding whether or not a formula was obvious would be an NP-hard problem and one would not be able to construct a quickly terminating procedure for deciding if a given formula is obvious (unless $P = NP$). However, refutation is included as an inference step in the high-level proof language. Thus any valid Boolean formula has a high-level Ontic proof.

The second collection of rules of obviousness involve equality.

- $\Gamma \vdash$ (= u u) for any expression u.
- If $\Gamma \vdash$ (= u v) then $\Gamma \vdash$ (= v u).
- If $\Gamma \vdash$ (= u v) and $\Gamma \vdash$ (= v w) then $\Gamma \vdash$ (= u w).
- If u and w are compositional applications (f $s_1 \ldots s_n$) and (g $t_1 \ldots t_n$) respectively, and $\Gamma \vdash$ (= f g) and for $1 \leq i \leq n$, $\Gamma \vdash$ (= s_i t_i), then $\Gamma \vdash$ (= u w).
- If u and w are λ-expressions with congruence combinator representations (K $s_1 \ldots s_n$) and (K $t_1 \ldots t_n$) respectively, and $\Gamma \vdash$ (= s_i t_i) for $1 \leq i \leq n$, then $\Gamma \vdash$ (= u w).
- If $\Gamma \vdash$ (= Φ Ψ) and $\Gamma \vdash \Phi$ then $\Gamma \vdash \Psi$.
- If $\Gamma \vdash$ (= Φ Ψ) and $\Gamma \vdash$ (NOT Φ) then $\Gamma \vdash$ (NOT Ψ).

The third and final collection of rules of obviousness for quantifier-free Ontic involves quotations. A quotation is a term of the form (QUOTE *symbol*) and each quotation should be viewed as a constant symbol. The constant symbols represented by quotations are subject to the constraint that no two of them can be equal.

Quotations:

- If c is a quotation then $\Gamma \vdash$ (IS c SYMBOL) for any premise set Γ.
- If c and d are two distinct quotations, and $\Gamma \vdash$ (= c d), then $\Gamma \vdash$ **FALSE**.

It is possible to prove that the inference relation defined by the rules of obviousness for quantifier-free Ontic is quickly decidable. The decision procedure is based on a combination of Boolean constraint propagation (which takes linear time) and congruence closure. The worst case running time of this combined procedure is dominated by the worst case running time of congruence closure. Assuming that hash table lookups take constant time, it is possible to determine whether or not $\Gamma \vdash^{\circ} \Phi$ in time proportional to $n \log n$ where n is total number of expressions that occur in Γ or Φ.[1] This $n \log n$ worst case behavior is due to the fact that the congruence closure algorithm is based on a simple $n \log n$ implementation of union-find. If a balanced-tree technique is used instead of a hash table, the worst case running time becomes $n \log^2(n)$. A more complete discussion of congruence closure is given in [DWNY80].

5.2   First-Order Rules

First-order Ontic is expressively equivalent to first order predicate calculus. In order to insure that one can quickly determine if a formula is provable under the rules of obviousness, certain rules must be carefully constrained. More specifically, one can not allow a rule of obviousness that states that if Φ is an obviously true universal statement then all possible instantiations of Φ are also obvious. If such an unrestricted rule was included then deciding whether a given equation obviously follows from a set of equational axioms would require the ability to solve arbitrary algebraic word problems — it is well known that no decision procedure for these problems can be constructed. However, to make the notion of obviousness useful in practice, some version of universal instantiation must be included in the rules of obviousness — there must be some way of applying universal facts from the lemma library in the process of deciding whether a given formula is obvious. Ontic's universal instantiation rule of obviousness is restricted so that universal statements can only be instantiated with focus objects.

The only true quantifier in the Ontic language is λ and the only rule of inference that instantiates quantifiers is β-conversion. For a particular λ-expression f, the inference rule of β-conversion corresponds to a universally quantified equation. More specifically, if f is the λ-expression (LAMBDA $(x_1^{\tau_1} \ \ldots \ x_k^{\tau_k}) \ b(x_1^{\tau_1} \ \ldots \ x_k^{\tau_k}))$, then the inference rule of β-conversion states that, for all $x_1^{\tau_1} \ldots x_n^{\tau_n}$, the application $(f \ x_1^{\tau_1} \ldots x_n^{\tau_n})$ equals $b(x_1^{\tau_1} \ \ldots \ x_k^{\tau_k})$. To insure that the notion of obvious derived from the rules of obviousness is decidable, the β-conversion rule of obviousness must be restricted. Inference rules that allow for the instantiation

---

[1]Note that the number of expressions that occur in Γ or Φ can be much smaller than the number of expression occurrences in Γ and Φ; a given expression may have many occurrences.

of variables can be restricted via the notion of a focus object. In general, a universal statement should be restricted so that it can only be instantiated with the focus objects of the context in which obviousness is being computed. For the β-conversion inference rule this means that an application of a λ-expression can not be β-reduced unless all of the arguments in the application are focus objects. In the following rules λ-functions and λ-type-generators are treated separately from λ-types.

λ-Functions and λ-Type-Generators:

Let f be a function or type-generator (LAMBDA $(x_1^{\tau_1} \ldots x_k^{\tau_k})$ b) and let $u_1 \ldots u_n$ be elements of the focus set $\mathcal{F}$. Let ω be the syntactic substitution containing the pairs $x_i^{\tau_i} \mapsto u_i$.

- If, for each argument u_i, we have $\Gamma, \mathcal{F} \vdash$ (IS u_i $\omega(\tau_i)$) then $\Gamma, \mathcal{F} \vdash$ (= (f $u_1 \ldots u_n$) $\omega(b)$)

For example, consider an expression (f c d) where f is a λ-function (LAMBDA $(x^{(\text{MEMBER-OF } s^{\text{SET}})}$ $s^{\text{SET}})$ b). To apply β-conversion to the expression (f c d) one must prove the type check formulas (IS d SET) and (IS c (MEMBER-OF d)). Note that the type (MEMBER-OF s^{SET}) which appears in the λ-function is replaced by (MEMBER-OF d) in the type checking formula. If the type-check formulas are obviously true, and c and d are members of the focus set, then the application (f c d) is obviously equal to b with x^{SET} replaced by d and $x^{(\text{MEMBER-OF } s^{\text{SET}})}$ replaced by c.

The above rules of obviousness only partially constrain the semantics of λ-functions and λ-type-generators. More specifically, the β-conversion rule only applies when the arguments are of the correct type; if the arguments are not of the correct type then the β-conversion rule does not place any constraints on the meaning of the application. In the Ontic system this ambiguity is left unresolved: all inference rules in Ontic remain sound under any convention for assigning semantic interpretations to applications of λ-functions and λ-type-generators to arguments of the wrong type.

Intuitively, an application of a λ-function or λ-type-generator to arguments of the wrong type is a semantically ill-formed expression. Whether or not a given application is semantically ill-formed may depend on the

interpretation of free variables. Thus a given expression may be semantically well-formed under one variable interpretation but semantically
ill-formed under a different interpretation. In Ontic there is a variety of
ways in which an expression can be semantically ill-formed. For example, a term of the form (THE τ) is semantically ill-formed unless there is
exactly one instance of the type τ. In general, the rules of obviousness
do not constrain the meaning of ill-formed expressions; the rules remain
sound under any interpretation of such expressions.

Unlike λ-functions and λ-type-generators, the semantics of λ-types are
fully specified. All instances of a λ-type of the form (LAMBDA (x^τ) Φ)
must also be instances of the type τ. Thus, if u is not an instance of the
type τ then the formula (IS u (LAMBDA (x^τ) Φ)) must be false. This
specification for λ-types is captured in contrapositive form in the rule of
obviousness for λ-types given below.

λ-Types:

Let σ be a λ-type (LAMBDA x^τ $\Phi(x^\tau)$).

- If u is a member of $\mathcal{F}$, and $\Gamma, \mathcal{F} \vdash$ (IS u τ), then

  $\Gamma, \mathcal{F} \vdash$ (= (IS u σ) $\Phi(u)$).

- If $\Gamma, \mathcal{F} \vdash$ (IS u σ) then $\Gamma, \mathcal{F} \vdash$ (IS u τ).

In addition to λ-expressions, the second layer of the Ontic language
contains existence-formulas. The meaning of existence-formulas is given
implicitly in the following rules of obviousness for existence formulas.

Existence Formulas:

- If $\Gamma, \mathcal{F} \vdash$ (EXISTS-SOME σ) then $\Gamma, \mathcal{F} \vdash$ (IS x^σ σ) where
  x^σ is any variable of type σ.

- If $\Gamma, \mathcal{F} \vdash$ (NOT (EXISTS-SOME σ)) then for any term u we
  have $\Gamma, \mathcal{F} \vdash$ (NOT (IS u σ)).

If a type expression denotes a non-empty type then the variables of
that type are guaranteed to denote instances of the type. On the other

hand, if a type expression denotes the empty type then it is impossible for any term to denote an instance of that type. Thus, if τ is an empty type, then x^τ can not denote an instance of the type τ and the formula (IS x^τ τ) must be false. If τ denotes an empty type then the variable x^τ is considered to be a semantically ill-formed expression; the Ontic inference rules are sound under any convention for assigning a meaning to x^τ in the case where τ denotes the empty type.

The classical inference rule of universal instantiation can be derived from the rules of obviousness for existence formulas, λ-expressions, and Boolean operators. The rule of universal instantiation states that if one can derive (FORALL (x^τ) $\Phi(x^\tau)$), and one can derive (IS u τ), then one can derive $\Phi(u)$. This inference rule can be derived from the above rules in the case where u is a member of the focus set $\mathcal{F}$. More specifically, suppose one can derive (FORALL (x^τ) $\Phi(x^\tau)$) and (IS u τ) where u is a member of $\mathcal{F}$. In Ontic the formula (FORALL (x^τ) $\Phi(x^\tau)$) abbreviates (NOT (EXISTS-SOME (LAMBDA (x^τ) (NOT $\Phi(x^\tau)$)))). The rule of existence utilization states that, for any type σ, if one can derive (NOT (EXISTS-SOME σ)) then for any term u one can derive (NOT (IS u σ)). If u is a focus object that can be proved to be an instance of type τ then the rules for λ-types can be used to derive an equation between the formula (IS u (LAMBDA (x^τ) (NOT $\Phi(x^\tau)$))) and the formula (NOT $\Phi(u)$). The inference rules for equality then allow one to derive (NOT (NOT $\Phi(u)$)), and thus $\Phi(u)$. The restriction on the first rule for λ-types yields an analogous restriction on the derived rule of universal instantiation; a universal formula can only be instantiated with members of the focus set $\mathcal{F}$.

The following rule of obviousness implicitly determines the meaning of definite description terms of the form (THE τ) where τ is a type expression. These rules only constrain the meaning of (THE τ) in the case where there is exactly one instance of the type τ. If τ is empty or has more than one instance then the expression (THE τ) is considered to be semantically ill-formed; the rules of obviousness remain sound under any convention for assigning meaning to expressions of the form (THE τ) in cases where τ is either empty or has more than instance.

As stated in the introduction to this chapter, certain expressions are associated with "auxiliary formulas". These formulas play a role in the network generation mechanism described in section 6.3. The following states a rule of obviousness and specifies the auxilliary formulas associated with a definite description term.

Definite Description:

If u is a term of the form (THE τ) then the auxiliary formulas for u are (FORALL (x^τ y^τ) (= x^τ y^τ)) and (FORALL (x^τ) (= u x^τ)) and we have the following rule of obviousness:

- If $\Gamma, \mathcal{F} \vdash$ (EXISTS-SOME τ) and $\Gamma, \mathcal{F} \vdash$ (FORALL (x^τ y^τ) (= x^τ y^τ)) then $\Gamma, \mathcal{F} \vdash$ (FORALL (x^τ) (= u x^τ)).

The next rule of obviousness implicitly determines the meaning of types of the form (RANGE-TYPE f).

Range Types:

Let σ be the type (RANGE-TYPE (LAMBDA ($x_1^{T_1}$ ... $x_k^{T_k}$) b)). The instances of the type σ are the possible values of the body b as the arguments ($x_1^{T_1}$ ... $x_k^{T_k}$) range over their associated types. The auxiliary formulas of σ are (FORALL ($x_1^{T_1}$ ... $x_k^{T_k}$) (IS b σ)) and (FORALL (x^σ) (EXISTS ($x_1^{T_1}$ ... $x_k^{T_k}$) (= b x^σ))).   For any premise set Γ we have the following two rules of obviousness:

- $\Gamma, \mathcal{F} \vdash$ (FORALL ($x_1^{T_1}$ ... $x_k^{T_k}$) (IS b σ))
- $\Gamma, \mathcal{F} \vdash$ (FORALL (x^σ) (EXISTS ($x_1^{T_1}$ ... $x_k^{T_k}$) (= b x^σ))).

The implicit specification of the meaning of first-order Ontic expressions can be completed with the addition of one more rule of obviousness. This rule of obviousness implicitly specifies the meaning of the type THING.

Thing:

- $\Gamma, \mathcal{F} \vdash$ (IS u THING) for any term u.

There are two sources of incompleteness in Ontic's notion of obviousness: the incompleteness of the rules of obviousness for Boolean connectives and the focus restriction on the rules for β-conversion. The high-level proof language compensates for these two sources of incompleteness by providing two rules of inference that are not included in the rules of obviousness. The first high-level rule is the refutation rule discussed in section 5.1. The second high-level rule is focus projection.

Focus Projection:

- If there exists a focus set $\mathcal{F}$ such that $\Gamma, \mathcal{F} \vDash \Phi$ then $\Gamma \vdash \Phi$.

The above rules of obviousness, together with the high-level rules of refutation and focus projection, seem to be "complete" for first order Ontic. Unfortunately, it appears to be difficult to prove a technical completeness result. The difficulty arises from the existence of semantically ill-formed expressions. Under any particular fixed semantic convention for assigning values to semantically ill-formed expressions there are true statements that can not be proven via the above rules. Thus, it would seem, the rules can not be complete. There are several approaches to solving this problem. First, one might add inference rules that remove the semantic ambiguity of semantically ill-formed expressions. In practice, however, one is only interested in semantically well-formed expressions and the extra inference rules for specifying the value of semantically ill-formed expressions would needlessly detract from the performance of the system. A second approach would be to somehow remove semantically ill-formed expressions from consideration in the completeness theorem. This is difficult because an expression may be semantically well-formed under one interpretation and yet semantically ill-formed in another interpretation. Any first order completeness theorem must allow for a large number of different interpretations and very few expressions involving non-logical constants are well-formed in all interpretations. A third approach is to change the fundamental concept of an interpretation so that, rather than consisting of a first order domain together with interpretations for non-logical constants, an interpretation is any function on syntactic expressions that satisfies certain recursive constraints. It seems likely that this approach would yield a completeness theorem that in some way captures the notion that the above rules are adequate. However, this highly non-standard notion of a semantic interpretation seems to undermine the significance of a completeness theorem. In spite of the technical difficulties involved in a proof of completeness, the above rules of obviousness, together with the non-obvious rules of refutation and focus projection, appear to be "complete" for first order Ontic.

This section presents two more rules of obviousness. These rules are redundant in the sense that any application of these rules can already be derived under the refutation and focus projection closure of the rules already given. However, these additional rules strengthen the notion of obviousness and thus reduce the length of many high-level proofs. These rules will be called "shortcut" rules because they shortcut the need for some refutation or focus projection step. The first additional rule of obviousness states that if u is obviously an instance of τ then τ is obviously non-empty. This inference could already be done via refutation: if τ were empty then one can derive (NOT (IS u τ)). Since refutation is not a rule of obviousness, however, the following rule of obviousness shortcuts the need for certain explicit steps in high-level proofs.

Witness Shortcut:

- If $\Gamma, \mathcal{F} \vdash$ (IS u σ) then $\Gamma, \mathcal{F} \vdash$ (EXISTS-SOME σ).

The final rule of obviousness in this section is universal generalization. In natural deduction systems for first order predicate calculus the inference rule of universal generalization states that if one can derive a formula $\Phi(x)$, and x does not appear free in any premise of the derivation, then one can also derive the formula $\forall x \Phi(x)$. Because of the nature of the typed variables in Ontic, one must be careful to insure that Ontic's universal generalization rule is sound. To state a sound universal generalization inference rule we need some additional definitions.

Definition: A variable x^τ is *constrained by* a set of formulas Γ if x^τ is a subvariable of some member of Γ.

Definition: A variable x^τ is *maximal* in an expression u if x^τ is not a subvariable of the type of any subvariable of u.

We can now state a sound universal generalization inference rule. It should be remembered that (FORALL (x^τ) $\Phi(x^\tau)$) is an abbreviation for (NOT (EXISTS-SOME (LAMBDA (x^τ) (NOT $\Phi(x^\tau)$))))). Thus the inference rule of universal generalization might also be called negative existential introduction.

Universal Generalization Shortcut:

- If $\Gamma, \mathcal{F} \vdash$ (NOT $\Phi(x^\tau)$), x^τ is not constrained by Γ, and x^τ is maximal in $\Phi(x^\tau)$, then

  $\Gamma, \mathcal{F} \vdash$ (NOT (EXISTS (x^τ) $\Phi(x^\tau)$)).

The restriction that x^τ be maximal in $\Phi(x^\tau)$ insures that the derived formula is syntactically well-formed in the sense of section 4.2. If β-conversions were computed using simple substitution then syntactically ill-formed expressions could be allowed in the language without much difficulty. However, the maximality restriction on universal generalization would still be needed to insure the soundness of the rule. If x^τ were not maximal then the formula $\Phi(x^\tau)$ can be written as $\Phi(x^\tau, y^\sigma)$ where x^τ is a subvariable of the type σ. More specifically, consider the formula

(IS x^{NUMBER} (LESS-THAN $y^{(\text{GREATER-THAN } x^{\text{NUMBER}})}$))).

This formula is true for any type-respecting interpretation of the variables x^{NUMBER} and $y^{(\text{GREATER-THAN } x^{\text{NUMBER}})}$. But consider the universal generalization

(FORALL $(x\ ^{\text{NUMBER}})$
   (IS $x\ ^{\text{NUMBER}}$
       (LESS-THAN $y\ ^{(\text{GREATER-THAN } x\ ^{\text{NUMBER}})}$)))).

Under the semantics described in chapter 4, this syntactically ill-formed universal formula is α-equivalent to

(FORALL $(z\ ^{\text{NUMBER}})$
   (IS $z\ ^{\text{NUMBER}}$
       (LESS-THAN $y\ ^{(\text{GREATER-THAN } x\ ^{\text{NUMBER}})}$)))).

But this universal statement is clearly false under any (necessarily fixed) interpretation of $y^{(\text{GREATER-THAN } x^{\text{NUMBER}})}$.

The universal generalization rule of obviousness is redundant in the sense that any application of this rule could have been derived using previous rules together with refutation and focus projection. The universal generalization rule is used to show that a certain λ-type is empty. The same inference can be made by first assuming that this λ-type is not empty and then focusing on a variable whose type is the λ-type in question. However, the universal generalization rule of obviousness appears to be very important in reducing the size of high-level proofs.

5.3   Set-Theoretic Rules

This section presents rules of obviousness related to set-theoretic Ontic. More specifically, this section presents rules of obviousness for reification expressions and range types. The focus set $\mathcal{F}$ is not used in the statement of these rules and will be left implicit as was done in section 5.1. The following rule of obviousness implicitly gives the meaning of reification expressions of the form (THE-SET-OF-ALL τ) as well as the meaning of the primitive type-generator MEMBER-OF. It also gives the auxiliary formulas associated with type reifications.

Set Reification:

If u is (THE-SET-OF-ALL τ), and τ is a small type, then the auxiliary formulas for u are (IS u SET) and (= (MEMBER-OF u) τ) and we have the following rules of obviousness:

- $\Gamma \vdash^{\circ}$ (IS u SET).
- $\Gamma \vdash^{\circ}$ (= (MEMBER-OF u) τ).

The following rule implicitly gives the semantics of reifications of functions as well as the semantics of THE-FUNCTION and RULE-DOMAIN.

Function Reification:

If u is the expression (THE-RULE f), and f is a small λ-function (LAMBDA (x^τ) b), then the auxiliary formulas for u consist of the formula (IS u RULE) and the equations (= (THE-FUNCTION u) f)

and (= (RULE-DOMAIN u) (THE-SET-OF-ALL τ)) and we have the
following rules of obviousness:

- $\Gamma \vdash$ (IS u RULE)

- $\Gamma \vdash$ (= (THE-FUNCTION u) f)

- $\Gamma \vdash$ (= (RULE-DOMAIN u) (THE-SET-OF-ALL τ)).

All of the rules of obviousness for the Ontic language have now been
presented. In addition to the rules of obviousness, the Ontic system
provides axioms which are included in the initial lemma library. These
axioms are discussed in the following section.

5.4   The Initial Lemma Library

The axioms in the initial lemma library serve two purposes. First, they
implicitly give the meaning of the Ontic constants, EITHER, SUBSET-OF,

```
(FORALL ((X THING) (Y THING)))
  (= (EITHER X Y)
     (LAMBDA ((Z THING))
       (OR (= Z X)
           (= Z Y)))))
(FORALL ((S SET))
  (= (SUBSET-OF S)
     (LAMBDA ((S2 SET))
       (FORALL ((X (MEMBER-OF S2)))
         (IS X (MEMBER-OF S)))))))
(FORALL ((S1 SET) (S2 SET))
  (= (RULE-BETWEEN S1 S2)
     (LAMBDA ((R RULE))
       (AND (= (RULE-DOMAIN R) S1)
            (FORALL ((X (MEMBER-OF S1)))
              (IS ((THE-FUNCTION R) X)
                  (MEMBER-OF S2)))))))
```

Figure 5.1
Axioms Describing Special Constants

```
(FORALL ((X SET) (Y (SUBSET-OF X)))
  (IMPLIES (IS X (SUBSET-OF Y))
           (= X Y)))
(FORALL ((R1 RULE) (R2 RULE))
  (IMPLIES (AND (= (RULE-DOMAIN R1)
                   (RULE-DOMAIN R2))
                (FORALL ((X (MEMBER-OF (RULE-DOMAIN R1))))
                  (= ((THE-FUNCTION R1) X)
                     ((THE-FUNCTION R2) X))))
           (= R1 R2)))
(EXISTS ((W SET))
  (AND (EXISTS-SOME (MEMBER-OF W))
       (FORALL ((X (MEMBER-OF W))
                (Y (MEMBER-OF W)))
         (IS (THE-SET-OF-ALL (EITHER X Y))
             (MEMBER-OF W)))))
(FORALL ((S SET))
  (EXISTS ((W (MEMBER-OF S)))
    (FORALL ((X (MEMBER-OF W)))
      (NOT (IS X (MEMBER-OF S))))))
(FORALL ((R RULE))
  (IMPLIES (FORALL ((X (MEMBER-OF (RULE-DOMAIN R))))
             (IS ((THE-FUNCTION R) X)
                 (LAMBDA ((S SET)) (EXISTS-SOME (MEMBER-OF S)))))
           (EXISTS ((R2 RULE))
             (FORALL ((X (MEMBER-OF (RULE-DOMAIN R))))
               (IS ((THE-FUNCTION R2) X)
                   (MEMBER-OF ((THE-FUNCTION R) X)))))))
```

Figure 5.2
Additional Axioms of Set Theory

and RULE-BETWEEN. These constants are all semantically equivalent to
certain syntactically large λ-expressions. The constants, however, are
classified as syntactically small and thus play an important role in incorporating axioms of set theory into the definition of syntactic smallness.
In addition to giving the meaning of certain constants, the axioms in
the initial lemma library contain certain axioms of set theory that are
not incorporated in the definition of syntactic smallness.

The axioms in Ontic's initial lemma library are shown in figures 5.1 and 5.2. For the sake of readability the axioms in the initial lemma library will be presented in the external syntax discussed in section 4.1.7. The axioms in figure 5.1 implicitly give the meaning of the constants EITHER, SUBSET-OF, and RULE-BETWEEN. The axioms in figure 5.2 encode additional principles of set theory. The first two axioms state extensionality principles for sets and rules: if two sets have the same members, or two rules have the same behavior as functions, then they are equal. The third axiom is a version of the axiom of infinity, it implies that infinite sets exist. The fourth axiom is a version of the so-called foundation axiom which implies, among other things, that no set can be a member of itself. The final axiom is a version of the axiom of choice.

All of the inference rules and initial axioms of the Ontic system have now been presented. The next section discusses the high-level proof language and the relationship between the rules of obviousness, high-level proofs and the non-obvious inference rules of refutation and focus projection.

5.5 High-Level Proofs

The rules of obviousness define an inference relation $\vdash$. Intuitively, the notation $\Gamma, \mathcal{F} \vdash \Phi$ means that Φ is obviously true in a context with premises Γ and focus objects $\mathcal{F}$. This notion of obviousness can be used as the basis for a high-level proof system where each step in high-level proof obviously follows from known lemmas and previous steps of the proof. The syntax of the high-level proof language has a simple recursive definition. However, not all syntactically legal proof expressions are correct; for a proof to be correct each step must obviously follow from known lemmas and previous steps.

The examples of proof expressions given in chapters 1 and 3 are somewhat different from the proof expressions described by in this section. This difference is due, at least in part, to differences between the external and internal Ontic languages as described in section 4.1.7. Proofs, like Ontic expressions, have both an external and an internal representation. The external language is needed because each internal Ontic variable includes its type as part of its syntax and it is quite difficult to read and write expressions in which every variable occurrence also includes an occurrence of the type of that variable. In the external language variables are symbols that inherit types from the context in which they appear. If τ is an external type expression then the external context-constructor expression (LET-BE X τ) is used to establish a symbol-translation mapping from the external symbol X to an internal variable $x^{\tau'}$ where τ' is the internal translation of τ. This external context constructor also causes the internal variable $x^{\tau'}$ to become a focus object. An external proof expression can be translated in a fairly straightforward way into an internal proof expression and external proof expressions will not be discussed further here. There is a simple recursive definition for internal proof expressions.

Definition: A *proof expression* is one of the following:

- An expression of the form (NOTE Φ) where Φ is a formula.

- An expression of the form (SUPPOSE Ψ P_1 ... P_n) where Ψ is a formula and each P_i is a proof expression.

- An expression of the form (FOCUS-ON s P_1 ... P_n) where s is a term and each P_i is a proof expression.

The correctness of a proof-expression is defined relative to a context. A context $\mathcal{C}$ consists of three parts: a lemma library Ω, a current supposition set Σ, and a set $\mathcal{F}$ of focus objects. The lemma library of a context is assumed to be a set of closed formulas, i.e., formulas with no free variables. If P is a proof expression that is correct in a context $\mathcal{C}$, then the result of executing the proof P is a new context $\mathcal{C}'$ that is identical to $\mathcal{C}$ except that the lemma library of $\mathcal{C}'$ includes new lemmas. The correctness of proof expressions and the result of executing a correct proof expression are defined simultaneously.

- A proof expression (NOTE Φ) is correct if Φ can be derived by refutation, i.e., $\Gamma \cup \{(\text{NOT } \Phi)\}, \mathcal{F} \vdash \textbf{FALSE}$ where Γ is the union of the lemma library and supposition set of the context. If the expression (NOTE Φ) is correct in a context then the execution of (NOTE Φ) in that context generates a new lemma. More specifically, the new lemma generated is the universal closure of the implication $\Sigma \Rightarrow \Phi$ stating that the suppositions of the current context imply the noted formula.

- A proof expression of the form (SUPPOSE Ψ P_1 ... P_n) is correct in a context $\mathcal{C}$ with supposition set Σ if each proof P_i is correct in the context $\mathcal{C}'$ that contains the supposition set $\Sigma \cup \{\Psi\}$ and the lemma library derived from executing the proofs P_j for $j < i$. In other words, the proofs P_1 ... P_n must be correct under the additional supposition Ψ where each proof P_i is allowed to rely on the results of the previous proof expressions. The lemma library that results from executing a proof of the form (SUPPOSE Ψ P_1 ... P_n) equals the lemma library that results from executing the steps P_1 through P_n.

- A proof expression of the form (FOCUS-ON s P_1 ... P_n) is correct in a context $\mathcal{C}$ with focus set $\mathcal{F}$ if each proof P_i is correct in the context $\mathcal{C}'$ that contains the focus set $\mathcal{F} \cup \{s\}$ and the lemma library derived from executing the proofs P_j for $j < i$. In other words, the proofs P_1 ... P_n must be correct with the additional focus-object s where P_i is allowed to rely on the results of the previous proof expressions. The lemma library that results from executing a proof of the form (FOCUS-ON s P_1 ... P_n) equals the lemma library that results from executing the steps P_1 through P_n.

The high-level proof language defines an inference relation $\vdash$ where $\Omega \vdash \Phi$ means that there exists some sequence of proof expressions such that executing those proofs in the context with lemma library Ω and no suppositions or focus objects results in the addition of Φ as a lemma. Actually, anything provable by a sequence of proof expressions is provable by a single proof expression, although in practice theorems are usually proved with a sequence of proof expressions. It is possible to show that if Φ has no free variables then $\Omega \vdash \Phi$ if and only if Φ can be derived from Ω using the rules of obviousness together with the rule of refutation and the rule of focus projection.

The specification of the Ontic inference system is now complete. The Ontic language has been defined; the rules of obviousness have been given; the initial lemma library has been specified; the syntax of high-level proofs has been defined; and the notion of correctness for high-level proofs has been specified in terms of the notion of obviousness. The following chapter discusses an implementation of these specifications.

6 The Implementation

The Ontic implementation is similar in spirit to semantic network mechanisms described by other researchers in artificial intelligence [FHLM79], [BRAC79], [BRAC85], [ETHR83]. The Ontic implementation uses a network, or graph-like structure, in which each node represents a particular expression of the Ontic language. Ontic's inference mechanism can be viewed as a process of label propagation on this network. The network construction process is bounded so that the network generated in attempting to answer any question of obviousness is always finite. This guarantees that the label-propagation inference process always terminates.

The notation $\Gamma, \mathcal{F} \vdash \Phi$ will be used to indicate that Φ can be derived by label propagation on the network generated for Γ, $\mathcal{F}$ and Φ. Ideally, one would like the implementation to be *network-complete*, i.e., if $\Gamma, \mathcal{F} \vdash\!\!\circ\ \Phi$ then the network generated for Γ, $\mathcal{F}$ and Φ should be large enough that $\Gamma, \mathcal{F} \vdash \Phi$. Unfortunately, network-completeness may be difficult to achieve; it may be the case that $\Gamma, \mathcal{F} \vdash\!\!\circ\ \Phi$ but the derivation of Φ involves formulas that do not correspond to labels on the finite network generated for Γ, $\mathcal{F}$ and Φ. In this case label-propagation will terminate without deriving Φ. In some cases, however, one can achieve network-completeness. More specifically, if the rule of universal generalization is removed from the rules of obviousness then one can prove network-completeness for a certain set of network generation rules. Since one can prove network-completeness for a network generation process that always produces a finite network, one can prove that the inference relation $\vdash\!\!\circ$ (without universal generalization) is decidable.

The rule of universal generalization is redundant in the sense that any theorem provable using a notion of obviousness that includes universal generalization can be proved using a notion of obviousness that does not include universal generalization; universal generalization is a "shortcut" rule whose only effect is to reduce the length of high-level proofs. Dropping universal generalization from the rules of obviousness results in a theoretically cleaner system in which the implementation exactly matches its specification in terms of the rules of obviousness. However, the reduction in the length of high-level proofs seems well worth the loss of the theoretical nicety of network completeness. While examples can be constructed where something derivable using the rule of universal generalization is not derivable by label-propagation on the incomplete network, examples of this behavior have not yet been encountered in practice.

The efficiency of the label-propagation inference mechanism can be greatly improved through amortization. There are two primary costs in determining if a formula is obvious. First, of course, Ontic spends time propagating network labels. Second, Ontic spends a significant amount of time allocating data structures that represent Ontic expressions, i.e., allocating new nodes in the network. The cost of label propagation, and especially the cost of network data structure allocation and initialization, can be amortized over the lifetime of the Ontic system. Once a node is allocated it is never removed and can thus be re-used in many contexts. The high-level proof language is designed to allow a maximum of amortization of label propagation. For example, in a proof expression of the form (SUPPOSE Φ P_1 ... P_n), each of the proof expressions P_j share the same supposition set; new labels created in response to adding the supposition Φ are only added once and remain active during the execution of each P_j.

The effectiveness of amortization is greatly increased through a new technique called *semantic modulation*. Semantic modulation is similar in spirit to certain inheritance and virtual copy mechanisms that have been discussed in the knowledge representation literature [FHLM79]. The basic intuition is that, rather than instantiate universal quantifiers with focus objects, one can represent general knowledge as statements about certain generic individuals. Focus objects then "inherit" information from the generic individuals. This inheritance is achieved by treating the generic individual nodes as variables that can be temporarily "bound" to focus objects. A binding between a generic individual and a focus object is represented as an equation between two nodes. This equation interacts with inference rules for quantifier-free logic and causes the focus object to become a "virtual copy" of the generic individual. The term semantic modulation derives from the intuition that one is controlling, or modulating, the semantic interpretation of a fixed generic individual. The semantic interpretation of a fixed generic individual changes from context to context.

The explicit instantiation of quantifiers with focus objects would result in a large number of new expressions. By avoiding such instantiations, the semantic modulation inheritance mechanism avoids the construction of these new expressions; instead of constructing new expressions, old expressions containing generic individuals are re-used as representations of expressions involving focus objects.

6.1   Label Propagation

The network constructed in the Ontic implementation can be viewed
as a rootless directed acyclic graph, or DAG, representing a set of expressions. In a DAG representation of expressions arcs go from each
expression to its immediate subexpressions. In the Ontic implementation the reverse of each such arc is also stored. If a formula of the form
(IS s τ) is represented in the graph then the arcs of the graph contain
a path from the node representing s to the node representing τ via the
node representing (IS s τ). Each node in the graph structure is implemented as a data structure that contains both pointers to other nodes
and information about the current labeling state of the node.

To simplify the discussion of the inference mechanism, we abstract
away from the details of the network structure and take the network to
be simply a finite set of Ontic expressions. The symbol Υ will be used
to denote a finite set of expressions; the set Υ will be called a network
and the expressions in the set Υ will often be called nodes.

A "label" on the network Υ is either a token attached to a node
or an arc between two nodes. There are three kinds of token labels.
First, there are truth tokens representing the constants true and false.
A given formula node may have one, neither, or both of the truth tokens
attached to it. In addition to truth tokens, there are color tokens. Color
tokens represent equations between nodes; two nodes with the same color
token attached to them are considered to be equal. The attachment of
color tokens to nodes is implemented with a version of the union-find
algorithm that runs in $n \log n$ where n is the number of nodes in Υ.
The congruence closure mechanism is built on top of this union find
algorithm and also runs in $n \log n$ time assuming that hash table lookups
take constant time. There is also a third kind of token label called an
existence token. Type nodes that are labeled with existence tokens are
known to be non-empty types. In addition to token labels there are
"arc labels" which connect two nodes of the network. Each arc label
represents an is-formula of the form (is s τ) where s is a term nodes
and τ is a type node.

The discussion of labels can be greatly simplified by viewing the set of
labels as a set of formulas. An attachment of a truth token to a formula

node Φ either represents the statement that Φ is known to be true, or represents the statement that Φ is known to be false. An attachment of color tokens represents a set of equations between nodes in the network. Attachments of existence tokens to type nodes represent formulas of the form (EXISTS-SOME τ). Finally, the arc tokens represent is-formulas of the form (IS s τ).

> **Definition:** A *label formula* for a set of expressions Υ is either
>
> - a formula in Υ
> - the negation of a formula in Υ
> - an equation between elements of Υ
> - a formula of the form (IS u τ) where u is a term in Υ and τ is a type in Υ
> - or a formula of the form (EXISTS-SOME τ) where τ is a type expression in Υ.

One can view Ontic's label propagation process as an inference process which monotonically derives label formulas using rules of inference. For any given finite set of expressions Υ, i.e. any network, and any set of premises Γ, one can define the final result of the label propagation process as follows:

> **Definition:** For any set Υ of Ontic expressions, and any label formula Ψ of Υ, the notation $\Gamma, \mathcal{F} \vdash_\Upsilon \Psi$ indicates that there exists a derivation of Ψ from Γ using the rules of obviousness given in chapter 5 where every formula appearing in the derivation of Ψ is a label formula of the network Υ.

The label propagation inference mechanism is restricted to label formulas for the finite network Υ. Since there are only finitely many label formulas for a finite network, label propagation on a fixed finite network always terminates. The above definition does not specify any way of generating a network Υ. Before specifying the network generation process, however, the basic label propagation process needs to be modified to allow for semantic modulation.

6.2   Semantic Modulation

Semantic modulation is an inheritance mechanism in which focus objects inherit information from *generic individuals*. If Υ is a network, i.e., a set of expressions, then any variable that is a member of Υ is called a generic individual in the network Υ. All general information known to hold for instances of the type τ must be explicitly stated about each generic individual x^τ of type τ in the network Υ. If s is a focus object, and the label propagation process has derived the formula (IS s τ), then one can "bind" a generic individual x^τ of type τ to the term s. When binding x^τ to s the Ontic system first records records the binding as a pair $x^\tau \mapsto s$. The accumulated set of such bindings forms a syntactic substitution ω. Rather than apply the substitution ω to generate new expressions, the system takes each binding $x^\tau \mapsto s$ in ω and asserts the label formula (= x^τ s). Congruence closure then causes any expression in Υ that involves x^τ to be equated with the corresponding expression involving involves s, provided the corresponding expression is already a member of the network Υ. Thus s inherits statements about x^τ. Intuitively, the semantic modulation mechanism controls (modulates) the semantic interpretation of a generic individual x^τ so that x^τ means different things in different contexts.

Semantic modulation requires all information known to hold for instances of a type τ to be explicitly stated about each generic individual of type τ. In particular, each λ-expression that takes an instance of type τ as an argument must be explicitly applied to the generic individual x^τ and the β-conversion rule must be applied to this application. Suppose f is the λ-function (LAMBDA (x^τ) $(g\ x^\tau\ x^\tau)$). Furthermore, suppose that x^τ, y^τ and z^τ are three variables (generic individuals) in Υ of type τ. Semantic modulation requires each of the following equations to be explicitly represented in the labeling of the network.

$$(=\ (f\ x^\tau)\ (g\ x^\tau\ x^\tau))$$

$$(=\ (f\ y^\tau)\ (g\ y^\tau\ y^\tau))$$

$$(=\ (f\ z^\tau)\ (g\ z^\tau\ z^\tau))$$

The semantic modulation inference mechanism allows the general equation to be "inherited" by several different focus objects; each focus object inherits the general equation from a different generic individual.

Generating these explicit equations requires an alteration in the rule of β-conversion. More specifically, focused β-conversion, as presented in section 5.2, is replaced by the rule of generic β-conversion given below. Before this rule is given, however, some additional terminology is needed.

An application of a λ-expression is called a β-redex. An is-formula of the form (IS u (LAMBDA (x^τ) $\Phi(x^\tau)$)) is considered to be an application of a λ-type and is also considered to be a β-redex. A β-redex is generic if each argument of the β-redex is a variable of the same type as the corresponding formal parameter of the λ-expression. For example, the expression ((LAMBDA (x^σ) b) y^σ) is a generic β-redex. In the case where there is more than one argument the type of one formal parameter may depend on the interpretation of another formal parameter. For example, let f be a λ-function (LAMBDA $(x^\tau$ $z^{(\text{GREATER-THAN } x^\tau)})$ b) where GREATER-THAN is some Ontic type generator defined on instances of type τ. The function f takes two arguments where the second must be greater than the first. A generic application of f is a generic β-redex of the form (f y^τ $s^{(\text{GREATER-THAN } y^\tau)})$ where the arguments y^τ and $s^{(\text{GREATER-THAN } y^\tau)}$ are both variables of the appropriate type. Note that the type of the second argument, (GREATER-THAN y^τ), is different from the type of the second parameter of f, (GREATER-THAN x^τ). However, the substitution induced by this β-redex is generic in the sense defined below.

> **Definition:** A *generic β-redex* is a β-redex with λ-expression (LAMBDA $(x_1^{\tau_1}$ ... $x_k^{\tau_k})$ b) and arguments $y_1^{\sigma_1} \ldots y_n^{\sigma_n}$ such that for each argument $y_i^{\sigma_i}$, the type expression σ_i equals the type expression $\omega(\tau_i)$ where ω is the substitution containing the pairs $x_i^{\tau_i} \mapsto y_i^{\sigma_i}$.

Generic β-Conversion:

- If v is a generic β-redex with λ-expression

  (LAMBDA $(x_1^{\tau_1}$ ... $x_k^{\tau_k})$ b)

  and arguments $y_1^{\sigma_1} \ldots y_n^{\sigma_n}$ then $\Gamma \vdash$ (= v $\omega(b)$) where ω is the syntactic substitution containing the pairs $x_i^{\tau_i} \mapsto y_i^{\sigma_i}$.

Note that the generic β-reduction rule is similar to the focus-restricted rules for λ-expressions given in chapter 5. The generic β-reduction rule differs from the focus-restricted rules in that the arguments of the β-redex must be generic individuals rather than focus objects.

Semantic modulation involves binding generic individuals to focus objects. This binding results in a semantic modulation substitution ω that maps generic individuals (variables) to focus objects. The process that generates the substitution ω is discussed in section 6.3. In this section we simply assume that some modulation substitution ω has been generated and define network label propagation in the presence of the substitution ω. This propagation is specified in a manner similar to the specification of label propagation in the absence of bindings. The notation $\Gamma \vdash_{\Upsilon,\omega} \Psi$ indicates that the label formula Ψ can be derived from the premise set Γ by label propagation on the network Υ in the presence of the substitution ω.

The semantic modulation substitution ω does not result in new network structure; it simply alters the label propagation process so that additional label formulas can be generated. More specifically, semantic modulation requires the generation of equations that "bind" a generic individual to a focus object. This binding operation can be specified as a rule of inference for label propagation.

Binding Introduction:

- If $x^\tau \mapsto s$ is a pair in ω then $\Gamma, \vdash_{\Upsilon,\omega} (= x^\tau\ s)$.

The soundness of label propagation under a semantic modulation substitution ω is justified in terms of a re-interpretation of the nodes in the network. In the presence of a substitution ω, each node s is interpreted as a representation of the expression $\omega(s)$. This will be called the ω-interpretation of the nodes in Υ. One further modification of the inference rules governing label propagation is required in order that propagation under ω-interpretation be sound: the restrictions on universal generalization need to be changed to take bindings into account.

Universal Generalization Under ω-interpretation:

Suppose $\Gamma \vdash_{\Upsilon,\omega} (\texttt{NOT}\ \Phi(x^\tau))$ and either x^τ is not mapped by ω or x^τ is mapped by ω but $\omega(x^\tau)$ is a variable. Let y^σ be $\omega(x^\tau)$ in the case where x^τ is mapped by ω and let y^σ be the variable x^τ in the case where x^τ is not mapped by ω.

- If

  - the formula (EXISTS (x^τ) $\Phi(x^\tau)$) is a member of Υ,[1]
  - y^σ is not constrained by Γ,
  - $\Gamma \vdash_{\Upsilon,\omega} (= \sigma \ \tau)$,
  - and there is no free variable z^ξ of $\Phi(x^\tau)$ other than x^τ such that y^σ is a subvariable of $\omega(z^\xi)$

  then $\Gamma \vdash_{\Upsilon,\omega} $(NOT (EXISTS ($x^\tau$) $\Phi(x^\tau)$)).

Note that the restrictions on the inference rule of universal generalization under ω-interpretation require that one determine if y^σ is a subvariable of $\omega(z^\xi)$. In the case where z^ξ is not mapped by ω, but some subvariable of ξ is mapped by ω, the expression $\omega(z^\xi)$ is defined to be some variable $s^{\omega(\xi)}$ of type $\omega(\xi)$. The definition of substitution insures that the variable $s^{\omega(\xi)}$ has an infinite index in the sequence of variables associated with the type $\omega(\xi)$. This, in turn, insures that this variable is not in Υ and not equal to the right hand side of any binding pair in ω. This allows one to determine whether or not y^σ is a subvariable of $\omega(z^\xi)$ without actually computing $\omega(z^\xi)$: for any variable y^σ in Υ, and expression s in Υ, y^σ is a subvariable of type $\omega(s)$ just in case one of the following conditions hold:

- y^σ is a free variable of s and y^σ is not mapped by ω.

- There exists a free variable z^ξ of s such that z^ξ is not mapped by ω and y^σ is a subvariable of $\omega(\xi)$.

- There exists a free variable z^ξ of s which is mapped by ω and y^σ is a subvariable of $\omega(z^\xi)$.

The above conditions specify a recursive procedure for determining if y^σ is a subvariable of $\omega(s)$ without computing the expression $\omega(s)$.

---

[1] When discussing the universal generalization inference rule we assume that all quantified expressions are canonicalized under α-equivalence so that the choice of the name of the bound variable is irrelevant.

Thus it is possible to check the restrictions on universal generalization without computing any substitutions. We can now formally define the result of label propagation on the network Υ under ω-interpretation.

> **Definition:** We write $\Gamma \vdash_{\Upsilon, \omega} \Psi$ if there exists a derivation of Ψ from Γ where every formula in the derivation is a label formula for the network Υ and where the rules of inference are modified so that the focus-restricted rules of chapter 5 are replaced with the generic β-conversion rule, universal generalization is replaced with universal generalization under ω-interpretation, and the additional rule of binding introduction is included.

Recall that, in the presence of a semantic modulation substitution ω, each node s is interpreted as a representation of the expression $\omega(s)$. The soundness of inference under ω-interpretation relies on ω satisfying certain conditions. The need for each condition on ω is discussed below.

> **Definition:** A substitution ω is *strictly non-circular* if, for each mapping $x^\tau \mapsto u$ in ω, no subvariable of u is mapped by ω.

> **Definition:** A substitution ω *preserves* a set of formulas Γ if no subvariable of an element of Γ is explicitly mapped by ω.

> **Definition:** A substitution ω is *well-typed* under a premise set Γ if, for each pair $x^\tau \mapsto u$ in ω, we have $\Gamma \vdash (\text{IS } u \ \omega(\tau))$.

> **Soundness Lemma:** If $\Gamma \vdash_{\Upsilon, \omega} \Phi$ and ω is strictly non-circular, preserves the formula set Γ, and is well-typed under Γ, then $\Gamma \vdash \omega(\Phi)$.

The semantic modulation mechanism, and the ω-interpretation of network expressions, are invisible to users of the Ontic system. The user-level behavior of the system is specified by the rules of obviousness and the specification of the high-level proof language given in chapter 5. To ensure that semantic modulation is hidden from the user, the Ontic implementation maintains certain invariants. More specifically, in the Ontic implementation a particular context in the execution of an external high-level proof contains a lemma library, a supposition set, a focus set, a semantic modulation substitution ω, and a symbol table ρ mapping external symbols to internal Ontic expressions. The Ontic implementation maintains the invariant that no subvariable of an element of the lemma library, supposition set, or focus set is mapped by the ω: the substitution ω preserves the lemmas, suppositions and focus objects. Furthermore, ω preserves all expressions that are the internal translation of any external expression; for any external symbol X such that $\rho(X)$ is defined, no subvariable of $\rho(X)$ is mapped by ω.

Although the semantic modulation substitution ω is invisible to the user, it plays a central role in determining if a given formula is obvious in a given context. For example, suppose u is a focus object of type τ and that there exists some λ-function f such that for any instance x^τ of type τ, $(f\ x^\tau)$ equals $(g\ x^\tau\ x^\tau)$. In the Ontic implementation the focus restricted inference rules of chapter 5 have been eliminated (and replaced by generic β-conversion). Thus, without any semantic modulation substitution, it would not be obvious that $(f\ u)$ equals $(g\ u\ u)$. However, given generic β-conversion, and thus the equation $(=\ (f\ x^\tau)\ (g\ x^\tau\ x^\tau))$, a semantic modulation binding containing the pair $x^\tau \mapsto u$ allows the implementation to derive the corresponding equation involving u. The advantage of semantic modulation over a more direct implementation of focused β-conversion lies in the amortization of label propagation and node allocation over different contexts. Generic β-conversion is more efficient because it only needs to be done once for each of a small number of generic applications. A single generic β-conversion equation can then be used in many different contexts under many different semantic modulation substitutions. Semantic modulation substitutions are more efficient than traditional substitutions because they do not require the allocation of new node structures; a semantic modulation substitution simply generates equations between existing variables and existing focus objects.

To prove the soundness lemma one must show that every rule of obviousness that operates under ω-interpretation preserves soundness in the sense given in the lemma, i.e., if Φ can be derived from Γ under ω-interpretation then $\omega(\Phi)$ can be derived from Γ. Several particular rules deserve mention. Section 5.1 contains a rule stating that if Ψ is a member of Γ then $\Gamma \vdash \Psi$. The soundness of this rule under ω-interpretation relies on the condition that ω preserves Γ. Section 5.2 contains a rule stating that if $\Gamma \vdash (\text{EXISTS-SOME } \tau)$ then, for any variable x^τ of type

$\tau, \Gamma \vdash$ (IS x^τ τ). The soundness of this rule depends on the fact that ω is well-typed. In particular, suppose that $\omega(x^\tau)$ is a term u. In this case $\omega(($IS x^τ $\tau))$ is the formula (IS u $\omega(\tau)$). The well-typedness condition on ω insures that this formula can be derived from Γ. The soundness of this rule under ω-interpretation also depends on the use of sophisticated rather than simple substitution in the statement of the soundness lemma. Suppose that x^τ is not directly mapped by ω. Recall that simple substitution has the property that if ω does not directly map x^τ then $\omega(x^\tau)$ equals x^τ. Sophisticated substitution, on the other hand, specifies that if x^τ is not directly mapped by ω then $\omega(x^\tau)$ is a variable of type $\omega(\tau)$. Now suppose that $\omega(\tau)$ is some type σ other than τ. Under sophisticated substitution, $\omega(($IS x^τ $\tau))$ is a formula of the form (IS y^σ σ) and one can establish soundness under ω-interpretation. Under simple substitution, however, $\omega(($IS x^τ $\tau))$ equals the formula (IS x^τ σ) and soundness fails.

Two more rules of obviousness under ω-interpretation deserve comment with respect to soundness. First, the soundness of universal generalization relies on reformulating the rule to take ω-interpretation into account. If (NOT (EXISTS (x^τ) $\Phi(x^\tau)$)) is derivable from (NOT $\Phi(x^\tau)$) under ω-interpretation then (NOT $\omega(($EXISTS (x^τ) $\Phi(x^\tau)$))) can be derived from (NOT $\omega(\Phi(x^\tau))$) using the ordinary rule of universal generalization. Second, the soundness of the rule of binding introduction relies on the fact that ω is strictly non-circular. The binding introduction rule states that if ω contains the binding $x^\tau \mapsto t$ then one can derive an equation between x^τ and t. If ω is strictly non-circular, and x^τ is bound to t, then $\omega(($= x^τ $t))$ is the formula (= t t) and the binding introduction rule is clearly sound.

6.3   Network Generation

When determining if Φ obviously follows from Γ under focus set $\mathcal{F}$, the Ontic implementation constructs a network Υ and a semantic modulation substitution ω. Semantic modulation is designed so that most of the network can be re-used in many contexts. In the Ontic system, once a given node data structure is allocated it is never de-allocated and thus the network grows monotonically over the lifetime of the system. In this section, however, the network generation process is described as a set of generation rules that construct a network for a particular set of premises Γ, focus set $\mathcal{F}$, and query-formula Φ. The Ontic system insures that the network used in a particular query always contains the network specified in this section.

The time required to determine if a formula is obvious to Ontic in a given context is strongly related to the size of the propagation network Υ. The rules for constructing the network represent a balance between the need to minimize the size of Υ for the sake of efficiency, and the desire for network-completeness. Recall that a network generation process is said to be network-complete if the network generation process insures that if $\Gamma, \mathcal{F} \models \Phi$ then $\Gamma, \mathcal{F} \vdash \Phi$. The unsubscripted relation $\vdash$ is defined at the end of this section, after the network generation process has been specified. If the shortcut rule of universal generalization is removed from the rules of obviousness then the network generation process described below can be shown to be network-complete. The details of the network generation process are largely motivated by the proof of network-completeness in the absence of universal generalization.

Network generation rules should not be confused with inference rules. Inference rules determine an inference process which generates label formulas for the members of the network Υ. Network generation rules are used to generate new nodes in the network Υ. Each network generation rule is expressed as a closure property on the set Υ. The first three closure properties are relatively simple.

> **Definition:** Υ is *subexpression closed* if for every expression u in Υ, and every free position p in u, the expression $p[u]$ is also in Υ.[2]

> **Definition:** Υ is *type closed* if for every variable x^τ in Υ, the type τ is also in Υ.

> **Definition:** Υ is *auxiliary-formula closed* if Υ contains all auxiliary formulas of all expressions in Υ.[3]

Subexpression closure is required to insure network-completeness relative to the quantifier-free rules of obviousness given in section 5.1. Type

---

[2] Free positions correspond to subexpressions that do not have free variables that are captured by quantifiers in the overall expression. Free positions are defined more precisely in section 4.3.

[3] Auxiliary formulas are defined in chapter 5.

closure is required to insure network-completeness relative to the λ-type inference rule and the witness shortcut rule of section 5.2. Auxiliary formula closure is needed to insure network-completeness with respect to inference rules that involve auxiliary formulas.

Two more network closure properties are given below: generic β-closure and binding-closure. These closure properties together insure network-completeness relative to the focus-restricted rules of chapter 5. To understand the generic β-closure property consider a λ-function f of the form $(\text{LAMBDA } (x^\tau) \ b(x^\tau))$. Suppose that Υ contains both the λ-function f and a variable (generic individual) y^τ of type τ. Generic β-closure requires that Υ also contains the application $(f \ y^\tau)$ as well as the β-reduct, $b(y^\tau)$, of this application. Given that these two expressions are in Υ, the rule of generic β-reduction will insure that they are equal. Intuitively, the generic β-closure property states that for each λ-expression f and each tuple of generic arguments to f, Υ must contains both the generic application of f and the β-reduct of that application.

Ontic λ-expressions can have more then one bound variable and one bound variable may appear free in the type of another bound variable. These fact make the formal statement of generic β-closure somewhat complex. Suppose f is a λ-function $(\text{LAMBDA } (x^\tau \ z^\xi) \ b)$ in Υ where x^τ appears free in the type ξ of the second bound variable. Now consider a variable y^τ of type τ such that y^τ is a member of Υ and let ω be the substitution consisting of the single pair $x^\tau \mapsto y^\tau$. Let ξ' be the type $\omega(\xi)$. If Υ contains a variable $s^{\xi'}$ of type ξ', then generic β-closure ensures that Υ also contains the generic β-redex $(f \ y^\tau \ s^{\xi'})$ where f is the above λ-expression. In addition, however, generic β-closure also ensures that even if Υ does not contain any variable $s^{\xi'}$ of type ξ', and thus no such generic β-redexes are generated, the network Υ must at least contain the type expression ξ'.

> **Definition:** A *partial generic application* of a λ-expression f is a variable substitution ω such that every variable directly mapped by ω is a bound variable of f and for each variable x^τ directly mapped by ω, $\omega(x^\tau)$ is a variable of type $\omega(\tau)$ and every free variable of τ that is a bound variable of f is also directly mapped by ω.

> **Definition:** Let f have the form $(\text{LAMBDA } (x_1^{\tau_1} \ \ldots \ x_k^{\tau_k}) \ b)$, let ω be a partial generic application of f, and let τ_i be the

type of a bound variable $x_i^{\tau_i}$ of f such that every free variable
of τ_i that is also a bound variable of f is mapped by ω. We
say that f and ω β-*generate* the type $\omega(\tau_i)$. If ω maps all
bound variables of f then we say that f and ω β-generate
both the generic β-redex with λ-expression f and arguments
$\omega(x_1^{\tau_1})\ldots\omega(x_n^{\tau_n})$, and the β-reduct $\omega(b)$ of this β-redex.

Definition: A set of expressions Υ is said to be *generically*
β-closed if, for every λ-expression f in Υ, and every partial
generic application ω of f such that for each variable x^τ
mapped by ω, $\omega(x^\tau)$ is in Υ, the set Υ also contains all
expressions β-generated by f and ω.

The network generation rules implicit in the above closure properties
are stated purely in terms of the network Υ. The fifth network closure
property, binding closure, involves both the focus set $\mathcal{F}$ and label formulas generated by the label propagation inference process. The binding
closure property reflects the fact that in the Ontic implementation the
network Υ is constructed on demand as new focus objects are introduced and new label formulas are derived. In addition to specifying
the generation of new network structure, the binding closure property
also specifies the construction of variable bindings. Recall that, in general, propagation takes place in the presence of a binding substitution
ω. Binding closure is a property of a pair $<\Upsilon,\omega>$ in the presence of a
premise set Γ and a focus set $\mathcal{F}$.

Definition: A pair $<\Upsilon,\omega>$ is said to be *binding closed* under
a focus set $\mathcal{F}$ and premise set Γ if for each focus object u in $\mathcal{F}$,
and for each type τ in Υ such that $\Gamma \vdash_{\Upsilon,\omega}$ (IS u τ), either
u is itself a variable of type τ, or the network Υ contains
a variable x^τ of type τ which is not a subvariable of any
element of Γ or $\mathcal{F}$, and such that the binding $x^\tau \mapsto u$ is a
member of ω.

Consider a premise set Γ and a focus set $\mathcal{F}$ that contains five terms
that are all provably instances of the type τ but that are not variables
of type τ. Also consider a pair $<\Upsilon,\omega>$ that is binding-closed for Γ and
$\mathcal{F}$. Since $\mathcal{F}$ contains five instances of τ that are not variables of type
τ, the substitution ω must contain five pairs of the form $x^\tau \mapsto u$. Since

a given variable can only be mapped once in a given substitution, the network Υ must contain at least five variables of type τ. Thus, implicit in the definition of a binding-closed pair $<\Upsilon, \omega>$ is a network generation rule for generating new variables in the network Υ; if $\mathcal{F}$ contains five instances of the type τ then Υ must contain five variables of type τ.

All the closure closure properties listed above can be combined to give the notion of a *complete* pair $<\Upsilon, \omega>$ where Υ is a network and ω is a variable substitution.

> **Definition:** A pair $<\Upsilon, \omega>$ will be called *complete* for a premise set Γ, focus set $\mathcal{F}$, and query formula Φ if Υ contains the members of Γ, $\mathcal{F}$, and Φ, no subvariable of Φ or a member of Γ or $\mathcal{F}$ is mapped by ω, Υ is free subexpression closed, type closed, defining-axiom closed, generic β-closed, and the pair $<\Upsilon, \omega>$ is binding closed under Γ and $\mathcal{F}$.

It is not immediately obvious that the network generation rules implicit in the above closure properties always generate a finite network. Fortunately, this can be proved.

> **Finite Network Lemma:** For any finite premise Γ, finite focus set $\mathcal{F}$, and goal formula Φ there exists a pair $<\Upsilon, \omega>$ such that both Υ and ω are finite, the pair $<\Upsilon, \omega>$ is complete for Γ, $\mathcal{F}$, and Φ, and the pair $<\Upsilon, \omega>$ is minimal in the sense that there is no pair $<\Upsilon', \omega'>$ that is complete for Γ, $\mathcal{F}$ and Φ such that Υ' is a proper subset of Υ or ω' is a proper subset of ω. The minimal complete pair $<\Upsilon, \omega>$ is unique up to the renaming of variables that are not subvariables of Φ or any member of Γ or $\mathcal{F}$.

The proof of the finite network lemma is quite long and cumbersome and is not given here. However, it should be noted that if the level of quantifier nesting in the formulas in Γ is bounded then the size of the generated network is linear in the number expressions that appear in Γ (either as elements or subexpressions of elements). This result is particularly important since, in practice, Γ contains a fairly large lemma library. In practice a good rule of thumb seems to be that the size of the generated network is proportional to $|\mathcal{F}|^3|\Gamma|$ where $|\mathcal{F}|$ is the number of focus objects in $\mathcal{F}$ and $|\Gamma|$ is the number of lemmas in the lemma library.

This rule of thumb corresponds to the assumption that most expressions in the network are generated by universal formulas in Γ that universally quantify over three variables. If there are n focus objects then, for each type τ, binding closure may generate n variables of type τ. If a lemma universally quantifies over three types, and there are n variables of each type, then generic β closure will lead to n^3 different copies of the body of the lemma. Thus if Γ consists of a large number of lemmas, each of which quantifies over three variables, then the number of nodes in the generated network is roughly n^3 times the size of Γ.

Given the notion of a complete pair $<\Upsilon, \omega>$ we can define the inference relation $\vdash$ implemented in the Ontic system.

> **Definition:** We write $\Gamma, \mathcal{F} \vdash \Phi$ if $\Gamma \vdash_{\Upsilon, \omega} \Phi$ where $<\Upsilon, \omega>$ is the minimal pair $<\Upsilon, \omega>$ complete for Γ, $\mathcal{F}$, and Φ.

The presentation of the relation $\vdash$ is now complete. Several theorems have been claimed without proof. First, it has been claimed that the network generation process is network-complete if universal generalization is removed from the rules of obviousness. Second, it has been claimed that, if the level of quantifier nesting in Γ is bounded, then the size of the generated network is linear in the size of Γ. Both of these theorems have quite long and cumbersome proofs which are not included here. It is unknown whether there exists a bounded network generation process that is network-complete when universal generalization is included in the notion of obviousness.

All of the technical definitions presented in this chapter are motivated by the desire to construct a faithful implementation of the high-level specification presented in chapter 5. The semantic network label-propagation mechanisms described in this chapter, including semantic modulation, seem to provide the best available implementation of the given specifications.

7 Conclusions

There are two ways of evaluating the ideas used in the Ontic system. First, one can attempt to evaluate the utility of the ideas in constructing useful systems. Second, one can attempt to evaluate the extent to which Ontic's inference mechanisms provide a plausible model of human mathematical cognition. This chapter addresses the first evaluation technique by presenting a list of potential applications of automated inference systems. These applications represent directions for future research; the limitations of Ontic's object-oriented inference techniques in these applications are not currently understood and future research may uncover other inference techniques that make these applications practical.

One potential application for automated inference systems is simply the verification of mathematical arguments; an author could increase his confidence in the correctness of a proof using machine verification. The time required to "debug" the formal representation of proofs in the Ontic system seems to make this application impractical at the current time. However, as the inference power of the system is increased, and the lemma library is made larger, machine verification of new mathematics could become practical.

Automated inference mechanisms are needed in the construction of interactive knowledge bases. The Ontic system is able to automatically use information from a lemma library. An Ontic system based on a lemma library that contained the contents of a mathematical textbook could answer certain questions about the contents of that book. Such an interactive textbook would be valuable in education. If the system could be made to run with a very large lemma library, a library containing the contents of many textbooks, one could construct an interactive mathematical encyclopedia. An interactive encyclopedia could be used by professional mathematicians to answer questions and verify arguments in domains that were not familiar to the human user.

Automated inference systems might also be useful in constructing interactive documentation systems. A computer operating system, for example, is usually associated with a large amount of documentation. One could translate this documentation into first order axioms that serve as a lemma library underlying an inference system. One would then have a device for answering questions about the documented system. The problem of answering questions about engineered devices seems similar to, but possibly more difficult than, the problem of answering questions about the material in a mathematical textbook.

Ontic's object-oriented inference mechanism could be applied to program verification. Ontic's type system is similar to the type systems of strongly typed programming languages. With sufficiently expressive types there is no distinction between type checking and verification; any verification problem for a computer program can be phrased as a type-checking problem. Ontic's object-oriented inference mechanisms are organized around types. It would be interesting to explore the application of Ontic's object-oriented inference mechanisms to program verification where verification is viewed as a form of type-checking.

Another possible application for Ontic's inference mechanisms is common sense reasoning. In his naive physics manifesto Hayes proposed writing down first order axioms that express common sense knowledge about the physical world [Hayes 85]. One might object to Hayes' proposal on the grounds that first order inference is intractable. It is clear, however, that certain limited inferences can be done quickly. It would be interesting to explore the application of Ontic's inference mechanisms to reasoning about common sense situations. Another objection to Hayes' proposal is that much, if not most, common sense reasoning is heuristic: the conclusions are not strictly implied by the given information. The heuristic nature of common sense reasoning does present a challenge to researchers attempting to build such systems and the integration of heuristic and mathematically sound reasoning seems like an important area for future research.

The following two sections explore particular potential applications in more detail. The final section of this chapter presents a summary of the Ontic System.

7.1   Interactive Knowledge Bases

Ontic's object-oriented inference mechanisms are designed to automatically access a large lemma library. By placing various kinds of information in the knowledge base underlying an Ontic-like system one could construct interactive mathematical textbooks, interactive mathematical encyclopedias, and interactive technical documentation libraries.

Access to information in Ontic's lemma library is controlled via types: the inference mechanism accesses only those portions of the lemma library that concern types that apply to the given focus objects. For example, when reasoning about graphs the system automatically ignores facts about differentiable manifolds. Thus the lemma library could include information about a large number of different subjects and still be used effectively.

There are several ways one could use an interactive mathematical encyclopedia. First, the encyclopedia could be used to answer questions about areas of mathematics that are unfamiliar to the user. Second, the encyclopedia could verify a user's argument. This would be especially useful when the human user is unfamiliar with the subject matter of his own argument. Finally, a mathematician who develops a new concept could ask the system if that concept has already been defined under some other name.

Recognizing user-defined concepts is particularly difficult; there may be a defined concept in the encyclopedia which is "essentially the same" as a user-defined concept but the two definitions are technically different. For example, consider the concept of an equivalence relation. An equivalence relation can be defined as a relation, i.e. a set of pairs, which is symmetric, transitive, and reflexive. Alternatively, an equivalence relation can be defined as a partition of a set into equivalence classes. These two definitions seem to define the same concept and yet the two classes are technically distinct: a partition is different from a set of pairs. Yet these two objects are in some sense the same; I will say they are *iso-ontic*.[1] There are many examples of iso-onticities. For example a function f of two arguments defines a Curried function f' such that for all arguments x and y, the application $f'(x)$ yields a function such that $f(x, y) = f'(x)(y)$. The function f is iso-ontic to its Curried version f'. As another example consider a graph. Another example is the definition of a topological space. A topological space can be defined as a pair of a set and s a higher-order predicate p such that for any subset u of s, $p(u)$ is true if and only if u is open. Alternatively, a topological space can be defined simply as a family of sets. An interactive knowledge base should recognize that these two definitions are equivalent; if a user defines a topological space in a way that is formally different from the definition in the knowledge base the system should still recognize the user's definition as a simple variant of the notion of a topological space,

---

[1]The term iso-ontic means "same being", or more loosely, equi-existent. For example, in any situation where an equivalence relation exists a partition also exists. This is different from the term isomorphic which means "same shape".

even though instances of the user's definition are unambiguously distinct objects from instances of the knowledge-base definition. Intuitively, a family of sets is iso-ontic to a certain set together with a higher-order predicate on subsets of that set.

Iso-onticity is not the same as isomorphism under the technical sense of isomorphism used by mathematicians. Intuitively, two objects x and y are isomorphic if there exists a bijection between between the "points" of the objects that "carries" the structure of x exactly onto the structure of y. If x and y are isomorphic then they must both have the same structure, e.g., they are both groups or both topological spaces or both differentiable manifolds. Iso-onticity, on the other hand, is a relationship that holds between objects of completely different structure, e.g., a family of disjoint sets (a partition) and a set of pairs (an equivalence relation). Although iso-onticity is not the same as isomorphism, it is possible to give a completely general formal definition of iso-onticity [McAllester 83]. Intuitively, the concept of iso-onticity is based on the idea of transforming one structure into another structure. For example, if P is a partition then one can define a transformation function f such that $f(P)$ is an equivalence relation. Intuitively, two objects, say a partition P and an equivalence relation E, are iso-ontic if there exists a transformation function f such that $f(P)$ equals E, and an inverse transformation g such that $g(E)$ equals P. Upon reflection, however, it is clear that for any two objects x and y there always exist mathematical functions (sets of pairs) f and g such that $f(x)$ equals y and $g(y)$ equals x. Thus, under a naive interpretation of iso-onticity, any two objects are iso-ontic. This problem can be overcome by distinguishing between essential and non-essential functions. Two objects x and y are iso-ontic if there exist *essential* functions f and g such that $f(x)$ equals y and $g(y)$ equals x. It now remains only to define the notion of an essential function.

In a foundational system such as Ontic all expressions are constructed from a few primitives. Furthermore, most expressions used in an actual proof contain free variables. Any proof about topological spaces starts by considering an arbitrary (or generic) topological space x^τ where τ is the type TOPOLOGICAL-SPACE. The vast majority of statements in an argument about topological spaces will contain free variables, either the generic topological space x^τ itself or some other variables whose type involves x^τ. A function expression that does not contain free variables,

i.e., a closed function expression, will be called essential. The notion
of an essential function can also be defined in a more semantic way by
stating that a function is essential if it commutes with automorphisms
of the foundational universe [MCAL83]. In practice, the syntactic definition of an essential function as a closed function expression is more
tractable. Two terms s and t (that each may contain free variables) are
provably iso-ontic if there exists *closed* function expressions f and g such
that the term $(f\ s)$ is provably equal to the term t and the term $(g\ t)$
is provably equal to the term s.

It seems likely that this notion of iso-onticity between terms can be
used in some way to recognize when two type expressions are "equivalent", e.g., are technically different versions of the single concept of a
topological space. The definition of equivalence for types can presum-
ably be based on some combination of the notions of isomorphism and
iso-onticity for terms. Ideally, the technical notion of equivalent types
should agree with human intuitions about equivalent definitions.

7.2   Software Verification

Type checking has proved to be a practical way of finding certain errors
in computer programs. Currently available type checking systems use
a weak vocabulary of types — there is no way to treat an arbitrary
predicate as a data type. If the type vocabulary is made richer then
stronger "semantic" properties of programs can be expressed as type
constraints. In fact, if any predicate on data structures can be expressed
as a type then any semantic specification for a computer program can
be expressed as type restrictions. For example, if iteration is replaced
by recursion then a programmer can provide loop invariants simply by
placing type restrictions on the arguments of recursive functions.

If arbitrary predicates on data structures can be expressed as types
then type checking requires theorem proving. One might argue that,
because theorem proving is intractable, one should not use fully expressive type systems. This criticism carries little weight, however, if one
is willing to allow type checking to fail. A failure to type check simply
means that the system failed to prove the program correct; it does not
mean that the program is wrong. Since Ontic's object-oriented theorem
proving mechanisms are guaranteed to terminate quickly, a type check-

ing system based on Ontic's theorem proving mechanisms could also be made to terminate quickly. One could give rules of obviousness for type checking that are analogous to Ontic's rules. These rules of obviousness would define the the notion of an obviously well-typed program. A programmer could be required to make sure that all his programs are obviously well typed. A correct program that is not obviously well-typed could be made obviously well-typed in one of two different ways. First, one could weaken the type restrictions on certain procedures. This corresponds to using a weaker type vocabulary such as the ones currently in use. Second, new lemmas could be asserted in the lemma library so that a the well-typedness of the procedure is obvious in the presence of these new lemmas.

Type checking has already been demonstrated to be practical for certain restricted type vocabularies. It seems likely that type checking using more expressive types would be equally practical in the sense that all programs that are well-typed under existing systems would correspond to obviously well-typed programs in the more expressive setting. In a more expressive setting, however, a programmer would be free to experiment with stronger type restrictions and with the statement of lemmas about stronger types that make his programs obviously well typed. In this more expressive setting the distinction between type checking and program verification would be eliminated and a programmer could select any degree of verification in the continuum between type checking and the full-blown verification of arbitrary loop invariants.

7.3   A Summary of Ontic

The Ontic system has many features not found in previous systems. Ideally, each new feature would be introduced and evaluated independent of the other features. For example, the uniform elimination of predicates in favor of types and type generators could be evaluated in a more traditional first-order framework, one independent of the axioms of set theory. Unfortunately, an independent evaluation of each individual new feature would be quite time consuming and would not properly account for synergistic interactions between various features. For example, the encoding of the set-theoretic axioms into a syntactic notion of smallness would be more cumbersome in a system that did not already have a rich type vocabulary. Although it is difficult to independently evaluate each individual feature of Ontic, it is possible to enumerate the novel features and to gain some intuition about the importance of each feature in the overall usefulness of the system. The Ontic system includes the following features.

- The Ontic formal language is organized around a rich vocabulary of types. The variety of ways types can be constructed interacts with the variety of ways types can be used resulting in the concise representation of a large variety of statements. Types can be constructed as λ-predicates, applications of type generators, or with the special type-constructor RANGE-TYPE. Types can be used to make formulas of the form (IS s τ), to restrict the range of quantifiers, to form a definite description term involving the THE, to form sets using the operator THE-SET-OF-ALL, or to express simple implications using the type-combinator macro IS-EVERY.

- Most of the axioms of Zermelo Fraenkel set theory are incorporated into the syntactic definition of a small type expression and a small function expression; type and function expressions which are syntactically small can be *reified* using the operators THE-SET-OF-ALL and THE-RULE respectively.

- Ontic provides a high-level proof language in which proof correctness is specified by a technical notion of an obviously correct step. The notion of obviousness is specified by inference rules called rules of obviousness.

- The high-level proof language allows for the explicit specification of certain terms, called focus objects, and the rules of obviousness are defined in terms of these focus objects. Thus we say that the high-level proof language and the rules of obviousness are both object-oriented.

- Ontic automatically finds and applies information from a large lemma library. It is possible to construct a decision procedure for the rules of obviousness that is capable of efficiently using all of the lemmas in a large lemma library when determining if a given statement is obvious.

- All Ontic variables include a type as part of their syntactic structure. This allows variables to play the role of Skolem witnesses for existential statements. It also allows variables to be used as generic individuals in the semantic modulation implementation. It further allows typed variables to act as arbitrary values in the universal generalization rule of obviousness; in universal generalization typed variables play the role of the Skolem constants in a resolution refutation proof that result from the negation of a universally quantified goal formula.

- Ontic's implementation of the decision procedure for the notion of obviousness is based on a semantic network style label-propagation technique. This mechanism allows a given node in the network structure to be re-used in many different contexts. The cost of label-propagation is also amortized over different contexts.

- Ontic's implementation of the rules of obviousness that involve focus is based on a semantic network style inheritance mechanism called semantic modulation. Semantic modulation avoids the construction of highly context-specific network structure by varying, or modulating, the semantic interpretation of fixed network structure. This is done by varying the semantic interpretation of certain variables called generic individuals. By allowing increased sharing of network structure and network labels, semantic modulation increases the effectiveness of the amortization of label-propagation over different contexts.

As of this writing it is not clear which of the above features are most responsible for the effectiveness of the Ontic system. It seems likely that all of the features contribute in some way. Future systems may incorporate new features such as new rules of obviousness, automatic type-checking, or tactics for automatically finding high-level proofs. In any case, I believe that progress in knowledge representation and machine reasoning is inevitable. Ultimately, such progress will have a profound effect on our society.

Bibliography

[AIT86]   Hassan Ait-Kaci, Roger Nasr, Logic and Inheretance, Thirteenth Annual
            Symposium on Principles of Programming Languages, January 1986, pp.
            219-228.

[ANDR81]   Peter Andrews, Theorem Proving via General Matings, JACM, Vol 28,
            no. 2, April 1981, pp. 193-214.

[BALL77]   A. M. Ballantyne and W. W. Bledsoe, Automatic Proofs of Theorems in
            Analysis Using Nonstandard Techniques, JACM vol. 24 no. 3, July 1977,
            pp. 353-374.

[BELL77]   John Bell and Moshe Machover, A Course in Mathematical Logic, North-
            Holland, 1977.

[BIBL79]   W. Bibel, Tautology Testing with a Generalized Matrix Reduction
            Method, Theoretical Computer Science 8, 1979, pp. 31-44.

[BIBL81]   W. Bibel, On Matrices with Connections, JACM vol. 28, No. 4, October
            1981, pp 633-645.

[BLED72]   W. W. Bledsoe, R. S. Boyer, W. H. Henneman, Computer Proofs of Limit
            Theorems, Artificial Intelligence 3, 1972, pp. 27-60.

[BLED73]   W. W. Bledsoe, Peter Bruel, A Man-Machine Theorem Proving System,
            Proc. of the 3rd IJCAI, 1973, pp. 56-65.

[BLED77]   W. W. Bledsoe, Non-resolution theorem Proving, Artificial Intelligence
            9, 1977, pp. 1-35.

[BOYR79]   Robert S. Boyer, J. Struther Moore, A Computational Logic, ACM
            Monograph Series, 1979.

[BOYR84]   Robert S. Boyer, J. Struther Moore, A Mechanical Proof of the Unsolv-
            ability of the Halting Problem, JACM, Vol. 31, No. 3, July 1984, pp.
            441-485.

[BOYR86]   Robert S. Boyer, J. Struther Moore, Overview of A Theorem-Prover for
            A Computational Logic, 8th International Conference on Autoated De-
            duction, Lecture Notes in Computer Science, Springer-Verlag 1986, pp.
            675-678.

[BUND73]   Alan Bundy, Doing Arithmetic with Diagrams, Proc. of the 3rd IJCAI,
            1973, pp. 130-138.

[BRAC79]   Ronald J. Brachman On the Epistemological Status of Semantic Net-
            works, in Readings in Knowledge Representation, R. Brachman, H.
            Levesque eds., Morgan Kaufmann Publishers, 1985.

[BRAC82]   R. Brachman, R. Fikes, H. Levesque, Krypton: A Functional Approach
            to Knowledge Representation, IEEE Computer 16, 1983, pp. 63-73

[BRAC85]   R. J. Brachman, J. Schmolze, An Overview of the KL-ONE Knowledge
            Representation System, Cognitive Science 9 (2), 1985, pp. 171-216.

[CARD84] Luca Cardelli, The Semantics of Multiple Inheritance, Procedings of the
          Conference on the Semantics of Datatypes, Springer-Verlag Lecture Notes
          in Computer Sciece, June 1984, pp. 51-66.

[CHAN73] C. Chang and R. C. Lee, Symbolic Logic and Mechanical Theorem Prov-
          ing, Academic Press, New York, 1973.

[CHOU84] Shang-ching Chou, Proving Elementary Geometry Theorems Using Wu's
          Algorithm, in Automated Theorem Proving after 25 Years, W. W. Bled-
          soe and D. Loveland eds., AMS Contemporary Mathematics Series 29
          (1984), 243-286.

[CHOU85] Shang-ching Chou, Proving and Discovering Geometry Theorems using
          Wu's Method. PhD thesis, Department of Mathematics, University of
          Texas, Austin (1985).

[CHOU86] Shang-ching Chou, William, F. Schelter, Proving Geometry Theorems
          with Rewrite Rules, Journal of Automated Reasoning 2, 1986, pp. 253-
          273.

[CNST82] R. L. Constable, S. D. Johnson, C. D. Eichenlaub, An Introduction to
          the PL/CV2 Programming Logic, Lecture Notes in Computer Science
          135, Springer-Verlag, 1982

[CNST85] R. L. Constable, T.B Knoblock, J. L. Bates, Writing Programs that
          Construct Proofs. Journal of Automated Reasoning 1 (1985) pp. 285-
          326.

[CNST85] R. L. Constable, Constructive Mathematics as a programming Logic I:
          Some Principles of Theory, Annals of Discrete Mathematics 24, North
          Holland, 1985, pp. 21-38

[CNST86] R. L. Constable, S. F. Allen, H. M. Bromely, W. R. Cleaveland, J. F.
          Cremer, R. W. Harper, D. J. Howe, T. K. Knoblock, N. P. Mendler, P.
          Panangaden, J. T. Sasaki, S. F. Smith, Implementing Mathematics with
          the Nuprl Development System, Prentice Hall, 1986.

[DAVS60] M. Davis and H. Putnam, A Computing Procedure for Quantification
          Theory. JACM 7 (March 1960), pp. 201-215.

[DAVS81] Martin Davis, Obvious Logical Inferences, Proc. of IJCAI-81, Vancouver,
          BC, August 1981, pp. 530-531.

[DBRJ68] N. G. de Bruijn, The Mathematical Language Automath, its use and
          some of its extensions. Symposium on Automatic Demonstration (VER-
          SAILLES, DECEMBER 1968), Lecture Notes in Mathematics, Vol 125,
          pp. 29-61, Springer-Verlag, Berlin, 1970.

[DBRJ72] N. G. de Bruijn, Lambda Calculus Notation with Nameless Dummies,
          Indagationes Mathematicae, Vol 34, pp. 381-92.

[DBRJ73] N. G. de Bruijn, The AUTOMATH Checking Project. Procedings of the
          Symposium on APL (Paris, December 1973), ed. P. Braffort.

[DKLR77] J. de Kleer, J Doyle, G. Steele, G. Sussman, Explicit Control of Reason-
          ing, MIT AI Lab. Memo 427, June 1977.

[DRSH79] Nachum Dershowitz, Orderings for Term Rewriting Systems, Proc. of the 20th Symposium on the Foundations of Computer Science, 1979, pp. 123-131.

[DWNY80] Peter J. Downey, Ravi Sethi, Robert E. Tarjan, Variations on the Common Subexpression Problem, JACM 27, No. 4, October 1980, pp. 758-771.

[ERNS73] G. W. Ernst, A Definition Driven Theorem Prover, Proc. of the 3rd IJCAI, 1973, pp. 51-55.

[ETHR83] David W. Etherington, Raymond Reiter, On Inheritance Hierarchies With Exceptions, AAAI-83, pp. 104-108.

[FHLM79] Scott E. Fahlman, NETL: A System for Representing Real World Knowledge, MIT Press, Cambridge Mass, 1979.

[GLRT59] H. Gelernter, Realization of a Geometry theorem Proving Machine, in Automation of Reasoning 1, J. Siekmann and G Writson (eds.) Springer-Verlag 1983.

[GLDS73] I. Goldstein, Elementary Geometry theorem Proving, MIT-AI Lab Memo 280, (April 1973).

[GRDN79] M. Gordon, R. Milner, C. Wadsworth, Edinburgh LCF, Lecture Notes in Computer Science 78, Springer-Verlag 1980.

[GRAT78] George Gratzer, General Lattice Theory, Academic Press, 1978.

[GTTG78] J. V. Guttag, J. J. Horning, The Algebraic Specification of Abstract Data Types, Acta Informatica 10, no. 1, 1978, pp. 1-26.

[HARP85] Robert Harper Aspects of the Implementation of Type Theory, Ph.D dissertation, Department of Computer Science Cornell University, 1985.

[HAYS85] Patrick Hayes, The Second Naive Physics Manifesto, in Formal Theories of the Commonsense World, J. Hobbs and R. Moore eds., Ablex Publishers, 1985.

[HOWE86] Douglas J. Howe, Implementing Number Theory: An Experiment with Nuprl, in 8th Internaltion Conference on Automated Deduction, Lecture Notes in Computer Science, Springer-Verlag, July 1986, pp. 404-415.

[HUET75] G. Huet, A Unification Algorithm for Typed ˇ-Calculus, Theoretical Computer Science 1, 27-57, 1975.

[HUET86] Gerard Huet, Theorem Proving Systems of the Formel Project, Proc. of the 8th International Conference on Automated Deduction, Lecture Notes in Computer Science, Springer-Verlag, 1986, pp. 687-688.

[HUET83] Gerard Huet, Jean-Marie Hullot, Proofs by Induction in Equational Theories with Constructors, JCSS 25, 1982, pp. 239-366.

[HGHS84] R.J.M. Hughes, The Design and Implemtation of Programming Languages, PhD Thesis, PRG-40, Programming Research Group, Oxford.

[INGS76] Daniel H. Ingalls, The Smalltalk-76 Programming System: Design and Implementation, 5th Annual ACM Symposium on Principles of Programming Languages, Jan. 1978, pp. 9-15.

[JTTG79] Checking Landau's "Grundlagen" in the AUTOMATH system. Mathematical Centre Tracts 83, Mathematisch Centrum, Amsterdam 1979.

[KAPR86] D. Kapur, G. Sivakumar, H. Zhang, RRL: A Rewrite Rule Laboratory, Proc. of the 8th International Conference on Automated Deduction, Lecture Notes in Computer Science, Springer-Verlag, 1986, pp. 691-692.

[KTNN84] Jussi Ketonen, EKL - A Mathematically Oriented Proof Checker, Procedings of the 7th International Conference on Automated Deduction, Lecture Note in Computer Science, 1984, pp. 65-79.

[KNTH69] Donald E. Knuth, Peter B. Bendix, Simple Word Problems in Universal Algebras, in Computational Problems in Abstract Algebra, J. Leech (ed.), Pergamon Press, 1969.

[KOZN77] Dexter C. Kozen, Complexity of Finitely Presented Algebras, Doctoral Dissertation, Computer Science Department, Cornell University, 1977.

[LSCN86] Pierre Lescanne, REVE a Rewrite Rule Laboratory, Proc. of the 8th International Conference on Automated Deduction, Lecture Notes in Computer Science, Springer-Verlag, 1986, pp. 695-696.

[LVSQ85] Hector J. Levesque, Ronald J. Brachman, A Fundamental Tradeoff in Knowledge Representation and Reasoning, in Readings in Knowledge Representation, R. J. Brachman, H. J. Levesque (Eds.), Morgan Kaufmann Publishers, 1985.

[LVLD78] Donald Loveland, Automated Theorem Proving: A Logical Basis, North-Holland 1978.

[LUSK82] E. L. Lusk, W. McCune, R. A. Overbeek, Logic Machine Architecture: Kernel Functions, Proc. of the 6th International Conference on Automated Deduction, Lecture Notes in Computer Science 138 (Ed. D.W. Loveland) Sprnger-Verlag 1982, pp. 70-84.

[LUSK84] E. L. Lusk, R. A. Overbeek, A Portable Environment for Research in Automated Reasoning, Proc. of the 7th International Conference on Automated Deduction, Lecture Notes In Computer Science, Springer-Verlag, 1984.

[MACK77] A. K. Mackworth, Consistency in Networks of Relations, Artificial Intelligence 8, 1977, pp. 99-118.

[MCAL83] David McAllester, Symmetric Set Theory, A General Theory of Isomorphism, Abstraction, and Representation, MIT AI Lab. Memo no. 710, August 1983.

[MCAL87] David A. McAllester, Ontic: A Knowledge Representation System for Mathematics, MIT AI Lab Technical Report 979, July 1987.

[MCDN84] J. McDonald, P. Suppes, Student Use of an Interactive Theorem Prover, in Automated Theorem Proving After 25 Years (W. W. BLEDSOE, D. W. LOVELAND EDS.), Vol 29 of Contemporary Mathematics, AMS, Providence R. I. 1984.

[MILL82] D. A. Miller, E. L. Cohen, P. B. Andrews, A look at TPS, Proc. of the 6th International Conference on Automated Deduction, Lecture Notes in Computer Science 138, Springer-Verlag, 1982, pp. 50-68.

[MURR82] N. V. Murray, Completely Non-Clausal Theorem Proving, Artificial Intelligence 18, 1982, pp. 67-85.

[NELS79] Greg Nelson, Derek Oppen, Simplification by Cooperating Decision Procedures, ACM Trans. Prog. Lang. Syst. 1,2 Oct. 1979, pp. 245-257.

[NELS80] Greg Nellson, Derek Oppen, Fast Decision Procedures based on Congruence Closure, JACM 27, No. 2, April 1980, pp 356-364.

[NEWL57] A. Newell, J. C. Shaw, H. A. Simon, Empirical Explorations with the Logic Theory Machine: a Case Study in Heuristics, in Automation of Reasoning 1, J. Siekmann and G Writson (eds.) Springer-Verlag 1983.

[NEVN74] A. J. Nevins, A human Oriented Logic for Automatic Theorem Proving, J. ACM 21, 1974, pp. 606-621.

[Nevins 75] A. J. Nevins, Plane Geometry Theorem Proving using Forward Chaining, Artificial Intelligence 6, 1975, pp. 1-23.

[ODON85] Michael J. O'Donnell, Equational Logic as a Programming Language, MIT Press, 1985.

[RETR73] R. Reiter, A Semantically Guided Deductive System for Automatic Theorem Proving, Proc. of the 3rd IJCAI, 1973, pp. 41-46.

[REYN74] J. C. Reynolds, Toward a Theory of Type Structure, in Colloquium on Programming, Lecture Notes in Computer Science, Volume 19, Springer-Verlag, 1974, pp. 408-423.

[REYN83] J. C. Reynolds, Types, Abstraction and Parametric Polymorphism, in Information Processing 83, R.E.A Mason, Ed, North Holland, 1983, pp. 513-512.

[ROBN65] J. A. Robinson, A Machine Oriented Logic based on the Resolution Principle, JACM 12, no. 1, 1965 pp. 23-41.

[RUSS85] David M. Russinoff, An Experiment with the Boyer-Moore Theorem Prover: A Proof of Wilson's Theorem, Journal of Automated Reasoning 1, 1985, pp. 121-139.

[SHNK85] N. Shankar, Towards Mechanical Metamathematics, Journal of Automated Reasoning 1, 1985, pp. 407-434.

[SHST82] Robert E. Shostak, Deciding Combinations of Theories, 6th International Conference on Automated Deduction, Lecture Notes in Computer Science, Springer-Verlag, 1982, pp. 1-12.

[SIEK83]   J. Siekmann, G. Wrightson ed., Automation of Reasoning: Classical Papers on Computational Logic, Springer-Verlag 1978 (in two volumes).

[SIEK84]   Jorg H. Siekmann, Universal Unification, Proc. of the 7th International Conference on Automated Deduction, Lecture Notes In Computer Science, Springer-Verlag, 1984.

[SIKL73]   L. Siklossy, A. Rich, V. Marinov, Breadth-First Search: Some Surprising Results, Artificial Intelligence 4, 1973, pp. 1-27.

[JONS87]   Simon L. Peyton Jones, The Implementation of Functional Programming Languages, Prentice Hall, 1987.

[SWRT77]   Stephen P. Schwartz, ed., Naming Necessity and Natural Kinds, Cornell University Press, 1977.

[SLAG74]   James Slagel, Automated Theorem-Proving for Theories with Simplifiers, Commutativity, and Associativity, JACM 21, No. 4, October 1974, pp. 622-642.

[STAL77]   Richard M. Stallman and Gerald J. Sussman, Forward Reasoning and Dependency-Directed Backtracking in a system for Compuer-Aided Circuit Analysis, Artificial Intelligence 9, 1977, pp. 135-196.

[STIC82]   M. Stickel, A Non-clausal Connection Graph Theorem Prover, Proc. of AAAI-82 National Conference on Artificial Intelligence, Pittsburgh, Pennsylvania, 1982, pp. 229-233.

[STIC85]   M. Stickel, Automated Deduction by Theory Resolution, Journal of Automated Reasoning 1, 1985, pp. 333-355.

[SUSS80]   Gerald J. Sussman, Guy Lewis Steele, CONSTRAITS — A language for Expression Almost-Hierarchical Descriptions, Artificial Intelligence 14, 1980 pp. 1-39.

[TRYB85]   A. Trybulec, H. Blair, Computer Assisted Reasoning with MIZAR, Proc. of IJCAI-85, Los Angeles, Ca., August 1985 pp. 26-28.

[TURN79]   David A. Turner, Another Algorithm for Bracket Abstraction, The Journal of Symbolic Logic 44, 2, June 1979, pp. 267-270.

[WLT84a]   Christoph Walther, Unification in Many Sorted Theories, European Conference on Artificial Intelligence, 1984, pp. 593-602.

[WLT84b]   Christoph Walther, A Mechanical Solution of Schubert's Steamroller by Many-Sorted Resolution, Procedings of AAAI-84, pp. 330-334.

[WLTZ75]   David L. Waltz, Understanding line drawings of scenes with shadows, in The Psychology of Computer Vision, Patrick H. Winston ed. McGraw-Hill, 1975.

[WEYH77]   Richard Weyhrauch, Arthur Thomas, FOL: A Proof Checker for First Order Logic, Stanford Artificial Intelligence Laboratory Memo AIM-235.1, 1977.

[WEYH80] Richard Weyhrauch, Prolegomena to a Theory of Mechanized Formal Reasoning, Artificial Intelligence, vol. 13 no. 1,2, April 1980, pp. 133-170.

[WOS82] L. Wos, Solving Open Questions with an Automated Theorem-Proving Program, Proc. 6th Conference on Automated Deduction, New York, Lecture Notes in Computer Science 138, Springer-Verlag 1982 pp. 1-13

[WOS84a] L. Wos, S. Winker, Open Questions Solved with the Assistance of Aura, in Automated Theorem Proving After 25 Years, Vol. 29 of Contemporary Mathematics (W.W. Bledsoe and D. W. Loveland Eds.), AMS, Providence, Rhode Island, 1984, pp. 73-88.

[WOS84b] L. Wos, R. Overbeek, E. Lusk, J. Boyle, Automated Reaoning: Introduction and Applications, Prentice-Hall, Englewood Cliffs, 1984

[WOS85] L. Wos, F. Pereira, R. Hong, R. Boyer, J. S. Moore, W. W. Bledsoe, L. J. Henschen, B. G. Buchanan, G. Wrightson, C. Green, An Overview of Automated Reasoning and Related Fields, Journal of Automated Reasoning 1, 1985, pp. 5-48.

[WU86] Wu Wen-Tsun, Basic Principles of Mechanical Theorem Proving in Elementary Geometries, Journal of Automated Reasoning 2, 1986, pp. 221-252

Index

Artificial Intelligence
Patrick Henry Winston and J. Michael Brady,
founding editors

J. Michael Brady, Daniel G. Bobrow, and Randall
Davis, current editors